ON FOOT
EAST SUSSEX DOWNS

18 short, medium and long walks
near Brighton, Eastbourne and Lewes

BEN PERKINS

S.B. Publications

By the same author:

South Downs: Walks for Motorists
Pub Walks in the South Downs
Village Walks in East Sussex
Waterside Walks in Sussex
Sussex Border Path: Guide and Map Pack
Classic Walks in Sussex

Contributed walks to:

Walkers Britain and Walkers Britain 2
AA Book of Village Walks
Exploring Britain's Long Distance Paths
AA Book of Family Walks

To Harry Comber

First published in 2000 by S.B. Publications
19 Grove Road, Seaford, East Sussex BN25 1TP
Revised and reprinted 2004

ISBN 1 85770 206 9

Typeset by Design 2 Output, Eastbourne.

Front Cover Photograph by Peter Lambert, Seaford.

CONTENTS

ACKNOWLEDGMENTS

The author is indebted to the Society of Sussex Downsmen for the use of part of the title of their original publication. *On Foot in East Sussex,* now out of print. Also, special thanks to Brian Ellis, who accompanied me on the walks, Ron Keen, Anne Lindfield and Roy Marchant, all experienced local walkers, who helped me decide which place and walks to include in this volume, and, even more difficult, which to leave out.

Front Cover: On the Seven Sisters, looking eastwards towards Birling Gap (Walk 7)

Back Cover: Alfriston and the banks of the Cuckmere river (Walk 8)

Title Page: Path on the flank of Bullock Hill (Walk 6)

Kingston from Kingston Hill. (Walk 17).

INTRODUCTION

It was almost 35 years ago, back in 1966, when a book called 'On Foot in East Sussex' first appeared in bookshops. Sponsored by the Eastbourne Rambling Club and financially supported by the Society of Sussex Downsmen, it was published at a time when public rights of way, even on the Downs, were poorly maintained and often difficult to follow. The walks were meticulously researched and written by a stalwart campaigner for rights of way, Harry Comber, who sought out many little used paths as well as more popular and established routes for inclusion in his book. I still have a well thumbed copy of that first edition which acted as a reliable guide to much of my downland walking at the time.

The book went through nine more editions, latterly under the banner of the Society of Sussex Downmen, before it finally ceased publication last year when Harry finally decided to hang up his boots.

Adopting part of the title, the present volume, produced with the blessing of Harry Comber and the Downsmen, attempts to fill the gap left by the demise of the original 'On Foot in East Sussex'. Although the walks are entirely new and only the downland area of East Sussex is covered, I happily acknowledge the inspiration and influence of the original 'On Foot'.

Everybody has a different image of the South Downs, but for many the term immediately conjures up the clean cut curves of the largely treeless Downs to the east of the River Adur, typified by the characteristic whale back profiles of Firle Beacon and Mount Caburn. The Downs within East Sussex lie within a reasonably compact area. To the west, on the county boundary, they form a narrow and vulnerable strip to the north of Brighton, already encroached upon by earlier housing developments, two universities and now threatened by a football stadium at Falmer. Further east, thinly populated and more secure from development, they widen to embrace a wide swathe of rolling open chalk hills which finally come to an abrupt end at the high chalk cliffs between Seaford and Eastbourne, forming the so-called Heritage Coast.

The six longer walks (numbered 13 – 18) have been designed to provide a broad survey of all the main areas of the Downs in East Sussex. They are substantial circuits, mostly across high hills with wide views. Although between 10 and 14 miles in length and sometimes fairly hilly, they offer fine exhilarating walking, mostly on good paths and tracks and firm underfoot. The medium length walks (numbered 7 – 12 and between 6 and 8 miles in length) fill in some of the gaps between the longer walks by visiting outlying areas such as Mount Caburn (Walk 9). Included in this group is a walk passing three of the villages on the 'spring line' where water bubbles out from under the chalk hills, at the foot of the Downs but still very much part of the downland landscape (Walk 10). The short walks (numbered 1 – 6 and between 3 and 5 miles in length) allow us to explore in more detail some of the finest areas in the Downs, such as the deserted and peaceful downland combes which can still be found within a mile or two of the coastal conurbation (Walks 3 and 6).

Thanks to the work of pioneer rights of way volunteer workers such as Harry Comber and, in recent years, a higher level of maintenance work by East Sussex County Council and, latterly, the Sussex Downs Conservation Board, most of the paths are in good order and well signed or waymarked. Although it should be possible to follow the walks using only the walk description and without a map, I would not recommend it. Features on the ground change unexpectedly, new fences, stiles and gates are erected and signposts and waymarks disappear. Luckily, the whole area covered by the walks in this book is included on two of the new OS Explorer maps (Nos 122 and 123) which, although large and cumbersome, have just the right amount of details for walkers. As new editions appear these maps will show public open access areas as well as rights of way.

While preparing the walk descriptions in this book, I have had an opportunity to visit almost every corner of this wonderful area. Although still largely unspoilt, it is nevertheless increasingly vulnerable to the pressures of modern life. The Brighton bypass has eaten into the already narrow strip of downland to the north of the coastal conurbation and the proposed football stadium at Falmer, seen as a fait accompli by many in spite of strong local opposition, would gobble up another precious piece of open downland. The Sussex Downs Conservation Board, although at present responsible for developing management plans for the Downs, lacks the power to resist developments supported by determined local authorities. In 1999 the government made the welcome announcement that it intends to create a new South Downs National Park. If implemented this may at long last give the area the protection it deserves.

If you would like to help protect the Sussex Downs, why not join the only independent organisation exclusively concerned with the preservation of the Downs. For more details of The Society of Sussex Downsmen, contact the Secretary at 10, The Drive, Hove, East Sussex BN3 3JA (Telephone: 01273 771906)

LOCATION OF WALKS

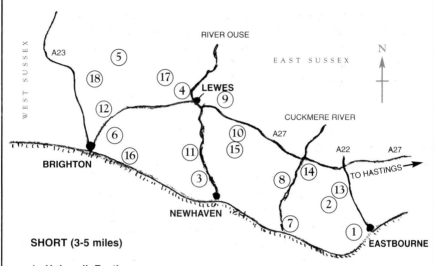

SHORT (3-5 miles)

1. Holywell, Eastbourne
2. Jevington
3. Piddinghoe
4. Offham-near-Lewes
5. Ditchling
6. Woodingdean
   (edge of Brighton)

MEDIUM (6-8 miles)

7. Exceat
8. Alfriston
9. Glynde
10. Firle
11. Southease
12. Ditchling Beacon

LONG (10-14 miles)

13. Butt's Brow, Willingdon
14. Wilmington
15. Firle
16. Rottingdean
17. Plumpton
18. Clayton Mills

Walk 1
HOLYWELL AND BEACHY HEAD

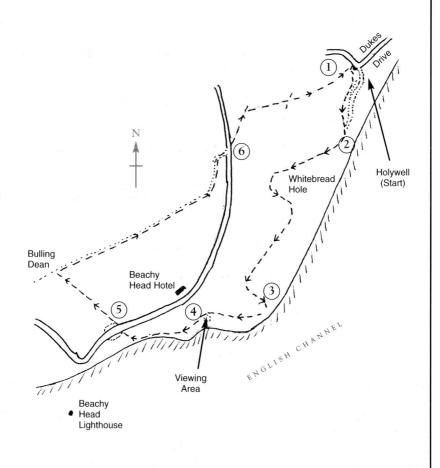

Walk 1
HOLYWELL AND BEACHY HEAD

Distance:	3³/₄ miles.
Route:	Holywell - Whitebread Hole - Beachy Head -Bulling Dean - Heathy Brow - Holywell.
Map:	OS Explorer 123: South Downs Way - Newhaven to Eastbourne.
Start/Parking:	At Holywell, at the far southwestern end of Eastbourne sea front. There is room to park in various places along Dukes Drive, as well as a handful of parking spaces next to the refreshment kiosk at Holywell where the walk starts and finishes (GR 600971).
Public Transport:	Bus from Eastbourne Town Centre.
Conditions:	The whole walk uses good paths or tracks, or crosses open downland pasture. One sharp climb up to Beachy Head.
Refreshments:	Pub and coffee shop at Beachy Head. Refreshment kiosk (seasonal) at Holywell.

For the first walk in this book, and one of the easiest, we travel to the far eastern end of the Downs where the high chalk ridge gives way to a final combe, Whitebread Hole, in the shadow of Beachy Head. After contouring round the lower slopes of this sheltered valley, a short sharp climb brings us to the summit of Beachy Head. The return route heads inland mainly across downland pasture managed by Eastbourne Borough Council.

THE WALK

Start the walk along a path which passes immediately to the right of the Holywell refreshment kiosk (1) (not the South Downs Way which goes straight up the hill). Our path climbs obliquely up to the left along the right of an area of scrub. Head for the sea, soon bearing right along the edge of the low scrub covered cliffs. Follow the cliff path down into Whitebread Hole. From the bottom (2), you can continue along the cliff path directly to point 3. Our described route, however, forks right along a more substantial track which skirts to the right of playing fields and contours round the lower hill side, much of it scrub covered but undergoing clearance to restore it, at least partially, to grass. The path finally turns towards the sea. At the cliff edge (3), turn right and climb steeply up on to Beachy Head.

At the top of this steep path a fenced viewing point provides our first glimpse of Beachy Head lighthouse, 142 feet high, built in 1902 to replace the older light at Belle Tout passed on Walk 13. The light has a range of 16 miles and is now, like almost all lighthouses, unmanned.

From here you should follow the South Downs Way along the cliffs and up to the highest point (4). Keep well away from the crumbling edge which is subject to frequent cliff falls. At the end of 1998 one of the biggest chalk falls ever recorded, occurred immediately above the lighthouse, almost filling the gap between cliff and lighthouse with chalk debris.

Beachy Head Lighthouse.

If in need of refreshment, the Beachy Head hotel is a few yards away to the right and has a bar and coffee shop. The whole area is a formidable tourist 'honey pot' which lovers of solitude will wish to avoid. The Beachy Head Countryside Centre next door could be worth a visit, particularly if you have children in tow. It offers several displays including a computer demonstration, a 3-D slide show featuring the wild life and history of the area and even a 'talking shepherd!' It is open daily from March to November and then at weekends until Christmas.

At the summit of Beachy Head, a small brick enclosure stands on the site of the former Lloyd's watch tower. The signal station operated until 1904, and was replaced by a large naval establishment. During World War II it was in use as a radar station of which, thankfully, no trace now remains.

Just past the signal station site, you will come to a plaque inscribed with a quotation from Psalm 93. At this point, veer half right across open downland, dropping down to reach the Beachy Head-to-Birling Gap road at a point where there are car parking areas on both sides of the road **(5)**. *Cross the road and follow a signposted bridleway which start from the right hand end of the car parking area and drops downhill, heading half left, undefined, across pasture. On reaching a fence, turn sharply back to the right. Follow this fence, keeping it on your left, down into a dip and up again. At the top, bear left with the fence out to join an access drive. Turn right for a few yards to join the Beachy Head road* **(6)**.

Cross the road and follow a signed bridleway, opposite, which heads out half left across pasture, a bit vague at first then as a more definite unfenced but trodden path. At a signpost, where Eastbourne comes into view ahead, bear half right, signed to the Sea Front. Another clear grassy path descends a ridge through thin scrub. The end of the walk soon comes into sight as you join the South Downs Way and follow it down to Holywell.

Walk 2
JEVINGTON, COMBE HILL AND WANNOCK

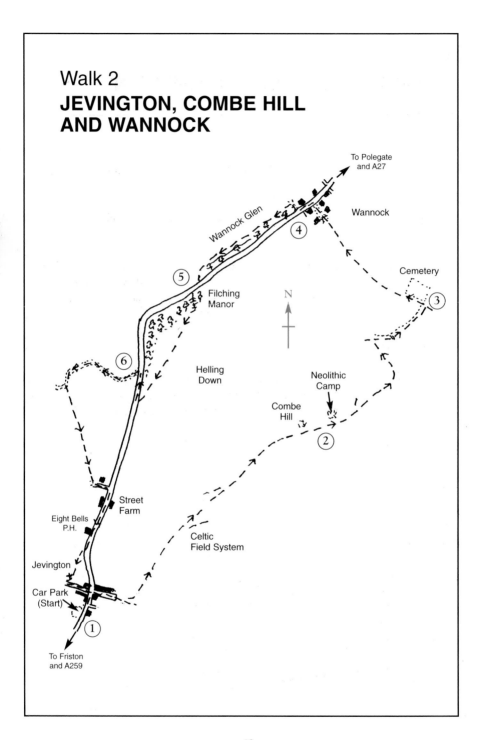

Walk 2
JEVINGTON, COMBE HILL AND WANNOCK

Distance:	4¹/₂ miles.
Route:	Jevington - Combe Hill - Wannock - Wannock Glen - Jevington.
Map:	OS Explorer 123: South Downs Way - Newhaven to Eastbourne.
Start/Parking:	At Jevington on the unclassified road linking the A27 at Polegate with the A259 coast road at Friston. The village car park is signed from the road at the southern edge of the village (GR 562012).
Public Transport:	None convenient.
Conditions:	One steep descent which may be slippery after rain. The path in Wannock Glen may also be muddy; otherwise mainly good 'going' across well drained chalk grassland.
Refreshments:	Pub and tea rooms at Jevington.

Seen at its best from the surrounding hills, Jevington nestles, half hidden by trees, in a secluded downland valley. It is a village without a central focus, spread out along the road for half a mile or more. The church, set back from the road on higher ground, is notable for its sturdy Saxon Tower with thick walls, suggesting that, when first built, it probably doubled as a refuge from Viking raiders. Inside, on the north wall of the Nave, look out for a fine Saxon sculpture of Christ's resurrection.

From the village, the walk climbs steadily to the summit of Combe Hill, a magnificent viewpoint, before dropping down to the edge of Wannock. A path then winds up the wooded Wannock Glen to Filching before crossing the shoulder of Helling Down back to Jevington. Towards the end of the walk you will pass the Eight Bells, a friendly pub which offers walkers a warm welcome.

THE WALK

From the entrance to the car park *(1)* turn left along the lane. Just short of the Hungry Monk restaurant, go right along Willingdon Lane, the second turning on the right. At the end of this cul-de-sac, go through a gate and immediately fork half left, signposted to Butt's Brow and also waymarked as part of the 1066 Country Walk. Follow a faint trodden path up the grassy hillside and on through an area of scrub.

You are passing through an ancient field system, a series of Lynchets or terraces running across the slope. They are not very obvious because of erosion and the partial covering of scrub.

A path continues up across an open area and in the same direction through a second belt of gorse and scrub where you should ignore all side paths. After a wide path joins from behind on the left, you will be following a section of another long distance route, the Wealdway. A wide unfenced path climbs steadily up to a stile and continues along the ridge of Combe Hill, passing several ancient barrows and, on the 638 foot summit, the ramparts of a Neolithic Camp.

Just before the path starts to drop down, it divides *(2)*. Fork left along a gently descending ridge path with superb views. At a four armed signpost, indicating steep and gentle routes down to Willingdon, go ahead along the gentle route which takes you on down the ridge before veering left on a broad grassy terrace. At a path T-junction, turn right and drop down with woodland on your left. After 100 yards or so, bear left down steps, through a swing gate and downhill along the left edge of pasture.

At the bottom field corner *(3)*, go left through another swing gate and ahead along the lower edge of a field with a small cemetery on your right. Continue in the same direction on a well worn path across two fields and then between fences to reach the road at the edge of Wannock.

Turn left and after 150 yards or so, just past a house with a beautiful garden called Broadwater, turn right along a farm track *(4)*. After 15 yards only, turn left along a narrow path, signposted to Jevington ½ mile although the actual distance is well over a mile. A narrow path squeezes along the left hand edge of several paddocks, with a stream in a wooded dip to your left and the road beyond. A path continues through Wannock Glen, a rather moist and, in summer, humid area of woodland, most uncharacteristic of the East Sussex Downs and a product of its sheltered position. The path brings you out after half a mile to the road opposite the entrance to Filching Manor.

The manor houses a Motor Museum. House and garden are open to the public from Thursday to Sunday during the summer months.

Turn right along the road until, after 100 yards *(5)* you can go left, steeply up through woodland where steps have been cut into the hillside. Once out of the wood, bear half right across downland. There is no defined path but you won't go wrong if you keep roughly parallel to the meandering fence boundary away to your right. Go over a stile in a crossing *fence and forward, now converging on the fence to your right. After about 150 yards, go over a stile in this fence to rejoin the road.*

Turn right beside this road, taking great care because of a combination of blind bend and steep banks with no verge. After a little over 200 yards (6) turn sharply back to the left on a track which climbs between banks. After 500 yards, turn left over a stile, go forward across grass and over two more stiles. Continue in the same direction down across a field with the houses on the edge of Jevington now in sight ahead. An enclosed path continues between paddocks to join a track where you should turn left out to a road.

Turn right into Jevington, passing the Eight Bells pub on your right. After another 100 yards a narrow path forks right and takes you to Jevington Church, where you will enter the churchyard through a centrally pivoted tapsell gate. Follow the church access drive back to the village street. Turn right back to the start.

Jevington Church.

Walk 3
PIDDINGHOE, NORE DOWN AND THE RIVER OUSE

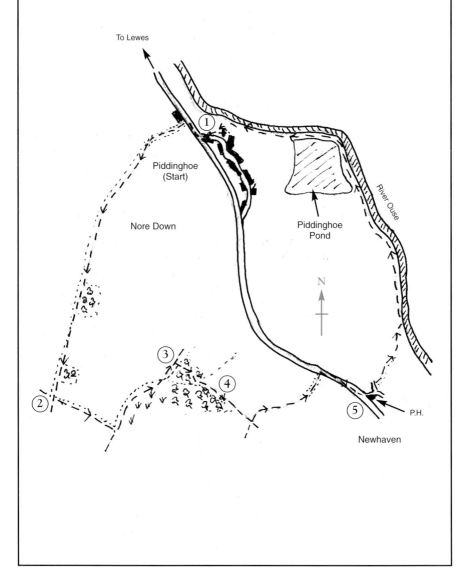

To Lewes

Piddinghoe
(Start)

Nore Down

Piddinghoe
Pond

River Ouse

N

P.H.

Newhaven

Walk 3
PIDDINGHOE, NORE DOWN
AND THE RIVER OUSE

Distance:	3³/₄ miles.
Route:	Piddinghoe - Nore Down - Bollen's Bush - edge of Newhaven - River Ouse - Piddinghoe.
Map:	OS Explorer 122: South Downs Way - Steyning to Newhaven.
Start/Parking:	The village of Piddinghoe on the Newhaven-to-Lewes road about a mile from Newhaven. There is limited roadside parking in the village street which forms a loop from the main road. The most unobtrusive roadside parking is at the Lewes end of the village street, just west of the church at GR 434031.
Public Transport:	Occasional weekday bus from Lewes or Newhaven.
Conditions:	Easy walking, mainly on good paths across gently undulating downland and along a raised river bank. One narrow path which may be overgrown - take a stick to beat down the nettles.
Refreshments:	Jolly Boatman pub on the edge of Newhaven at point 5. NB. The pub marked on OS maps at Piddinghoe is now closed.

This walk samples a precious area of downland to the north of Peacehaven, squeezed on all sides by development and vulnerable to more. It starts from the tiny village of Piddinghoe (pronounced locally as Piddennoo) beside the River Ouse. The church is notable for its round Norman tower, one of three in the Ouse valley. The other two, at Southease and in Lewes are set in a straight line, significant for students of Ley Lines. The trout weathervane on the church tower became the 'begilded dolphin' of Kipling's poem 'Sussex'. If you can get inside (the church was locked when I was there), seek out the 13th Century font and a 19th Century barrel-organ.

The walk climbs quickly out of the valley to cross undulating downland almost to the northern fringe of Peacehaven before turning to drop down to the edge of Newhaven. The last mile follows the bank of the River Ouse back to Piddinghoe.

THE WALK

Walk back to the Lewes end of Piddinghoe village street **(1)** *and turn right along the main Newhaven-to-Lewes road. After a few yards turn left through a wooden gate where there is a waypost indicating a public path to Peacehaven. A narrow grassy path squeezes between hedge and fence, It may be encroached upon by vegetation, particularly in the summer as it climbs steadily up on to the Downs.*

Beyond a stile, a view opens up to the left across the Ouse valley to Newhaven with Seaford Head in the background and a glimpse of Peacehaven ahead. From this point you get a good idea of how this green area is being pressed on all sides by housing development.

Follow an undulating headland path generally southwards for three-quarters of a mile. Towards the end, walk parallel to two sets of power lines and pass to the right of a block of woodland. Where the power lines dip underground at two substantial power poles **(2)**, *go over a stile in the field corner and immediately turn left on another headland track which crosses a valley with a hedge, left and the edge of Peacehaven a decent distance away to your right.*

About half way up the hill, immediately after entering an area of gorse and scrub, turn left on a track which runs along the hill side, a few yards inside this area of scrub, soon climbing gently. Once out into a field, go ahead along the right field edge.

After 150 yards **(3)** *turn right along a waymarked path which tunnels through scrub. Where this path divides, fork left, dropping down through more substantial woodland. At a T- junction* **(4)** *bear right uphill along a right field edge with woodland on your right.*

As you climb, another fine view opens out, back across the Ouse valley to Piddinghoe and beyond, through the Ouse gap, to the hills behind Lewes. From the top of the rise Newhaven is spread out ahead of you.

Just beyond the highest point, at a way post, turn left on a path within a grassy strip between two fields which becomes a hedged path and brings you down to the Lewes-to-Newhaven road where you should turn right. After 350 yards, just short of the 'Jolly Boatman' pub **(5)**, *fork left and immediately go left again along Robinson Road. After 40 yards fork left along a path and, after another 10 yards, fork right on a path which soon runs between a stagnant drainage channel on your left and an industrial boatyard area on your right.*

After 250 yards you can climb up onto the chalk embankment to your right and join a path along this raised Ouse river bank. Follow the river upstream for over a mile back to Piddinghoe. As you approach the village the path squeezes between the river and Piddinghoe pond, popular with sailors and wind surfers as well as the occasional heron and cormorant.

Piddinghoe Church.

River Ouse, Piddinghoe.

Walk 4
OFFHAM, MOUNT HARRY AND BLACKCAP

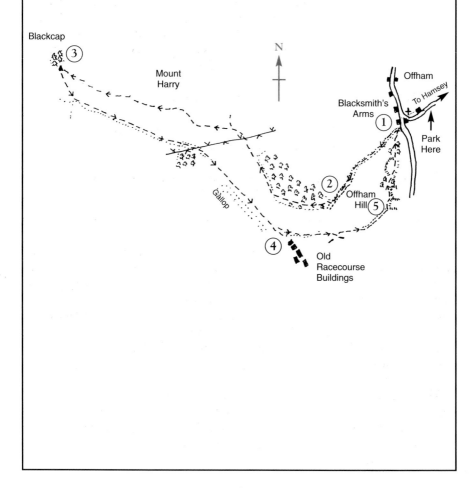

Walk 4
OFFHAM, MOUNT HARRY AND BLACKCAP

Distance:	4¹/₄ miles.
Route:	Offham - Mount Harry - Blackcap - Old Lewes Racecourse - Offham Hill - Offham.
Map:	OS Explorer 122: South Downs Way - Steyning to Newhaven.
Start/Parking:	At Offham on the A275 Lewes-to-East Grinstead road about a mile north of Lewes. There is safe roadside parking at GR 401122, about 200 yards along the unclassified road, signposted to Hamsey which leaves the A275 next to Offham Church.
Public Transport:	Hourly bus service from Lewes.
Conditions:	Mostly on excellent tracks or paths, also across open grass downland at Blackcap.
Refreshments:	Blacksmith's Arms pub at Offham just along the road from the start.

The tiny hamlet of Offham is tucked under the Downs, squeezed between the river and the wooded downland escarpment on the east side of the Ouse valley to the north of Lewes. The walk uses a well graded cart track up the flank of Offham Hill, gaining height without major effort. After leaving the woods, a less restricted path crosses Mount Harry before opening out on to an area of National Trust grass land. A short climb brings us to Blackcap, a fine viewpoint. Now growing towards maturity, the tree clump on the summit looks uncannily like that most famous of Sussex landmarks, Chanctonbury Ring before it was virtually destroyed in the Great Gale of 1987.

The return route passes near the old Lewes racecourse, where the buildings have been converted for residential use. To get back down to Offham we use a convenient permissive path, not marked on the OS map, which winds down through an area of old chalk quarries, now mellowing into a very pleasant green area with fine views from a plateau overlooking the Ouse valley.

THE WALK

Return to the A275 (1) and turn left. After less than 100 yards, go right along a rough track where a waypost indicates a bridleway to Blackcap. After a few yards, fork right along a chalky track which soon begins to climb steadily up on to the Downs.

You will soon find yourself walking parallel and to the right of a deep hollow way which looks as if it must have been the original access route on to Offham Hill, though it is now no longer an official right of way.

After about a quarter of a mile (2), leave the main track by side stepping to the right through a bridle gate and continue through woodland, ignoring a signed path to the left. The bridleway leaves the wood and continues along its top edge. Beyond the next bridle gate, go forward, parallel to a fence on the left, ignoring a right fork. Your route, marked at intervals with blue arrows, crosses more open ground, passes under power lines and continues gently up on to Mount Harry between patches of scattered gorse.

Once up to the highest point, your next objective, the clump of trees on Blackcap, comes into view ahead. Follow an unfenced path up across open ground to the summit (3).

From the trig point on the top, reverse your steps for a few yards only before diverging to the right of the route by which you reached the summit. Follow another clear track which takes you back across the right shoulder of Mount Harry.

The view from here is an exceptional one. Ahead you can pick out Malling Hill above Lewes with Mount Caburn beyond. Behind Caburn, on the other side of the Glynde Gap, is the instantly recognisable shape of Firle Beacon. Ahead and to the right, Seaford Head appears as a distinctive notch to the left of the Seaford/Newhaven gap at the mouth of the Ouse. Away to the right, a wide sweep of the downs escarpment between Kingston and Newmarket Hill complete the panorama.

The track picks up a fence on the right, passes through two gates and back under power lines. Beyond an area of scrub you will find yourself walking parallel to a gallop on your right. As you approach the old racecourse buildings. (4). Fork left on to a bridleway along the right hand edge of open ground with a post and rail fence on your right.

Beyond a bridle gate, where you have a choice of tracks, fork left again. Beyond the next bridle gate, go ahead, walking for a few yards parallel to a road on your right. Go forward through a second bridle gate and on with a fence on your left.

From this path there is another fine view to your right across Lewes, set against a backdrop of Mount Caburn to the right and Cliffe Hill to the left.

Where the fence bears half left, go with it, walking along the left hand edge of a large open public access area. In the field corner (5), go through a bridle gate and after 10 yards, turn left along a path which follows the rim of a disused quarry. At a waypost, fork right along a path which drops fairly steeply down through woodland and crosses an artificial plateau, a legacy of old quarry workings, overhung with chalk pits.

This striking amphitheatre, once an unnatural industrial intrusion, has now softened and mellowed into an acceptable feature of the landscape. The view from the edge embraces Lewes and a wide segment of the Ouse valley. The prominent church on a low mound in the foreground marks the site of the 'lost' village of Hamsey.

From the other side of the plateau a path continues down to join the A275 at the point where you left it at the start of the walk.

Offham Church.

Blackcap.

Walk 5
DITCHLING AND DITCHLING BEACON

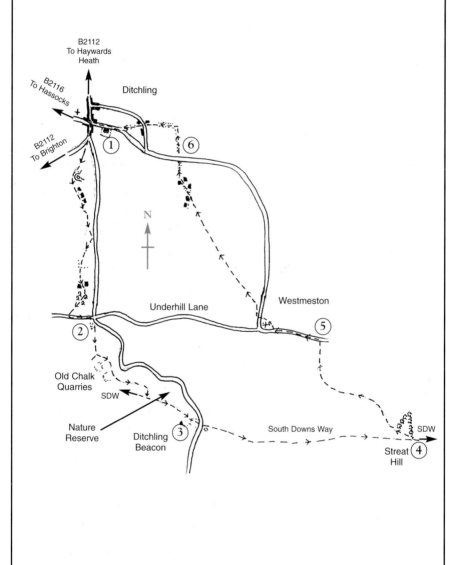

Walk 5
DITCHLING AND DITCHLING BEACON

Distance:	5 miles.
Route:	Ditchling - Ditchling Beacon - Streat Hill - Westmeston - Ditchling.
Map:	OS Explorer 122: South Downs Way Steyning to Newhaven.
Start/Parking:	Car Park behind Ditchling Village Hall, signposted to the south of the B2116 road to the east of the cross roads in the centre of the village of Ditchling (GR 327151).
Public Transport:	Infrequent weekday bus service from Lewes or Burgess Hill.
Conditions:	Field paths in the Weald; steep path up to the Beacon, may be slippery after rain, South Downs Way section mainly across firm, well drained downland pasture.
Refreshments:	Pubs and tea rooms at Ditchling. Ice cream van frequently parked at Ditchling Beacon car park.

This popular circuit links the village of Ditchling, at the foot of the Downs, with the summit of Ditchling Beacon. At 813 feet above sea level, this is one of the highest points on the South Downs and also an exceptional viewpoint. Inevitably, you will have to contend with a steep climb but it is well graded as it winds up through a nature reserve. You will be rewarded, not only by the views but also, a splendid walk along a fine open stretch of the South Downs Way between Ditchling Beacon and Streat Hill.

The walk description starts at Ditchling village, but if, like me you prefer to come across a pub half way round a walk, it would be perfectly feasible to start and finish the walk at the Ditchling Beacon car park, picking up the route description from point 3.

However you plan the walk, allow time to explore the village of Ditchling, perched on a low greensand hillock about a mile from the foot of the Downs escarpment. The 13th - 15th Century church, cruciform in shape, has a central tower surmounted by a so-called 'Sussex Cap'. Opposite the church, along the street to the west of the village cross roads, is a fine 16th Century brick and half timbered manor house, one of several given by Henry VIII to his fourth wife, Ann of Cleves. Nearby, next to the picturesque village green and pond, is a small museum, focusing on local history, but also displaying paintings by local artists. Additionally, during the summer months the museum mounts a series of special exhibitions.

THE WALK

From the entrance to the car park **(1)**, turn left. At the cross roads in the centre of the village, turn left. Shortly, at a road junction, take a narrow path which goes directly ahead between the two roads, signposted to the Downs. On reaching an estate road, skirt to the right of a roundabout and immediately turn right between gardens.

Once out into a field continue ahead over a footbridge. The path veers to the left across a field and them aims for the Downs. Continue, passing a wood and Park Barn Farm on your left out to join Underhill Lane, with the Downs escarpment looming up rather formidably in front of you. Turn left.

Just short of a road junction **(2)**, turn right across a small car park to enter a footpath which climbs steeply within the right hand edge of a belt of scrub. Beyond a stile you will come to a sign indicating that you are entering a Sussex Wildlife Trust nature reserve. From here you have a choice of paths, both of which will take you to the top of the Downs and both of which offer splendid routes. The more easily graded is the one that starts up steps to the left and through an area of old quarry workings.

Whichever path you choose, at the top bear left to join the South Downs Way and follow it up to the 813 ft summit of Ditchling Beacon. Details of the view from the top can be found in Walk 18.

Ditchling Village from Ditchling Beacon.

Dew Pond, Ditchling Beacon.

Walk past the trig point, a few yards away to your right and out through the Beacon car park.

*From the entrance to the car park **(3)**, cross the road and follow the South Downs Way eastwards, leaving a nicely restored dew pond on your right. A path, fenced on the right only, takes a fine unrestricted route between widely spaced fences along the top of the Downs escarpment. Follow the South Downs Way over the first rise and up to the top of a second incline, Streat Hill.*

*As the path begins to drop down again **(4)**, go left through a bridle gate, doubling back along a waymarked bridleway with the village of Ditchling in direct line ahead at first. It soon becomes a fine terraced bostal path which drops down, passing above a V-shaped clump of trees, planted to mark Queen Victoria's jubilee in 1887.*

With the aid of the map, you should be able to pick out, within the wide Wealden panorama, five churches at Ditchling, Streat, Plumpton, Westmeston and East Chiltington.

*From the bottom of the steepest slope a clear path, muddy in places, takes you out to the B2116 road **(5)**. Turn left along the new Jubilee pathway which takes you along the left hand side of the road. From this path, cross the road into Westmeston churchyard through a gateway next to a bus shelter.*

The church, although heavily restored, has fragments dating back to the 12th

Westmeston Church.

Ditchling Beacon from Streat Hill.

Century. The 17th Century brick porch incorporates timber dating from three hundred years earlier.

A path passes round behind the church and leaves the churchyard down steps in the far right corner. A short path takes you out via an access drive to rejoin the B2116. Turn right and after 10 yards, fork left on a path which climbs to the top of the roadside bank at first. Cross the drive to April Cottage and go over a stile.

Your path back to Ditchling now takes a straight line, obliquely across a number of fields, punctuated by stiles and waymarks, immaculately maintained by members of the so-called Monday Group of local volunteers. At one point the path passes through two deer enclosures, where gates have been provided in the high fences. Further on walkers seem to favour a gap in a hedge to the left of the stiled path but the official route provides the drier option.

At the edge of Ditchling an enclosed path squeezes between gardens, crosses an estate road and continues as a narrow path between wall and hedge. At the B2116 (6), go left for 15 yards, then right through a gate and ahead along the left edge of a playing field, passing behind the cricket pavilion. Pass between a tennis court and a children's play area, turn left through a gate and go forward along an access drive;. Cross a lane and follow the signed path opposite which brings you out via another access drive to the B2116. Turn right for a few yards back to the start.

Walk 6
STANDEAN BOTTOM AND CASTLE HILL

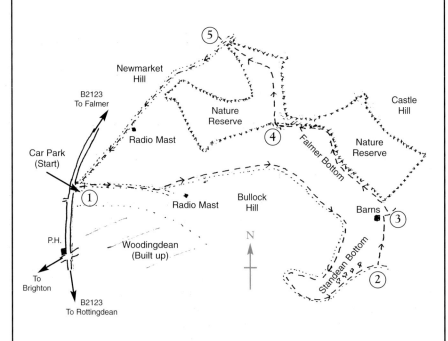

Walk 6
STANDEAN BOTTOM AND CASTLE HILL

Distance:	4¹/₂ miles.
Route:	Sunblest Bakery (disused) - Standean Bottom - Falmer Bottom - Castle Hill Nature Reserve - Newmarket Hill - Sunblest Bakery.
Map:	OS Explorer 122: South Downs Way - Steyning to Newhaven.
Start/Parking:	At the car parking and picnic area to the east of the B2123 Falmer-to-Rottingdean road, to be found immediately to the north of the built up area of Woodingdean and the disused Sunblest Bakery buildings. (GR 357064).
Public Transport:	Bus to Woodingdean from Brighton Town Centre.
Conditions:	An easy walk, entirely along firm chalk and flint tracks or grassy paths. No severe gradients.
Refreshments:	None on the route; pub at the road junction on B2133, about quarter of a mile south of the start.

Although never more than a mile from the edge of the densely built up Brighton suburb of Woodingdean, this walk takes you into a completely different world of solitude and tranquillity, cut off from the noise and pollution of the urban fringe. Starting across high ground, we follow a beautiful winding path down into Standean Bottom, a secluded dry downland valley. The return route winds up through the Castle Hill National Nature Reserve.

Leased from the owners, Brighton Borough Council in 1975, the Reserve covers almost 200 acres of rich chalk downland, some of which has probably never been ploughed. This undisturbed ground supports, in some areas, 30 different plant species in a single square metre, including many different grasses and several wild orchids, including the fragrant and spotted varieties which flower in June. Later, during July and August, you can seek out some less common downland flowers such as the round headed rampion, adopted as the emblem of the Society of Sussex Downsmen.

THE WALK

From the far the end of the car park (1), where you have a choice of two tracks ahead, take the one on the right which crosses high ground, running parallel to the built up area of Woodingdean, about 150 yards away to the right. After about 600 yards, fork left, go through a bridle gate and forward along a pleasant grassy track with a fence on your right and the hillside dropping away to your left. The path soon becomes a wide terraced track which takes a winding course, dropping very gently down for a mile and a half into Standean Bottom. Towards the bottom of the hill, the track is lined by a row of mature trees, a rare sight in the generally bare and open downland of East Sussex.

At a Y-junction of tracks in the valley (2), fork left. Pass to the right of a group of partially derelict barns, go through a bridle gate and turn right with a fence on your right. After 40 yards, at a way post (3), turn squarely left on an indistinct unfenced track which follows the right hand side of the floor of a side valley, Falmer Bottom. Beyond a bridle gate, the track is more definite, with a grassy bank rising up to the right. High on the hill across the valley to your left, you can pick out the terraced track used earlier in the walk. After about two thirds of a mile (4), go right through a bridle gate, following the direction of a waymark and passing to the left of a Castle Hill Nature Reserve notice.

The notice encourages walkers to stay on the public bridleway, a very reasonable request since this is such a sensitive nature conservation site. If you wish to visit other parts of the Reserve, contact the site manager at English Nature, (Sussex Office), 30 High Street, Lewes, Tel: 01273 476595, who offers occasional guided tours of the area. The boundaries of the Reserve are indicated on the walk sketch map.

An unfenced track takes you up through the reserve to a T-junction at the top of the hill (5). Turn left here and follow a clear track up past the ugly radio mast on the summit of Newmarket Hill and back to the start.

Standean Bottom.

Castle Hill.

Walk 7
EXCEAT, EAST DEAN AND THE SEVEN SISTERS

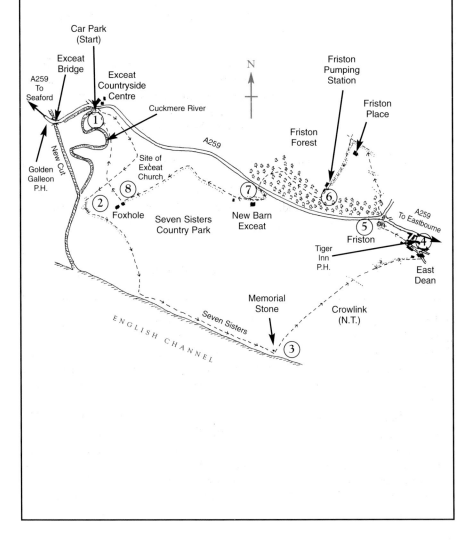

Walk 7
EXCEAT, EAST DEAN AND THE SEVEN SISTERS

Distance:	8 miles.
Route:	Exceat - South Downs Way - Cliff End - Seven Sisters - Crowlink - East Dean - Friston - Friston Forest - New Barn, Exceat - Seven Sisters Country Park - Exceat.
Map:	OS Explorer 123: South Downs way - Newhaven to Eastbourne.
Start/Parking:	At the Seven Sisters Country Park on the A259 Seaford-to-Eastbourne road where it drops down into the Cuckmere valley. The car park is to the south of the road opposite the Exceat Farm Countryside Centre at GR 514993. There is a charge for parking.
Public Transport:	Regular bus service from Eastbourne.
Conditions:	Much of the walk crosses firm well drained open downland; fairly hilly, particularly the switch back traverse of the Seven Sisters. The forest paths on the return route may be muddy.
Refreshments:	Tea rooms at Exceat Farm; Tiger Inn at East Dean.

In 1971, East Sussex County Council, aided by government grants, bought 692 acres on the eastern slopes of the lower Cuckmere valley which had previously been allowed to degenerate into an unsightly caravan and camping site. The outcome was the development of the Seven Sisters Country Park, now managed by the Sussex Downs Conservation Board to retain a balance between conservation and recreation.

The walk is a variant of a popular circuit which appeared in later editions of 'On Foot in East Sussex.' It not only explores the Country Park but provides a fine traverse over more than half of the Seven Sisters and a fine walk across the high open downland of Crowlink, a large National Trust area of preserved pasture downland. After visiting East Dean, providing a link point with Walk 13, the return route passes through the edge of Friston Forest before re-entering the Country Park.

THE WALK

At the entrance to the car park **(1)**, turn right along the A259. After a few yards, next to a bus stop, turn right. Go through a bridle gate and immediately bear left, signposted as the South Downs Way and Park Trail. Follow a clear terraced grassy path up on to Exceat Hill. Where it divides, fork right, keeping to the lower path, still on the South Downs Way which you will be following for the next 2¹/₂ miles.

At the top of the hill, a few yards to the left of the path, a stone marker stands on the site of the 'lost village' of Exceat, a casualty of the Plague epidemic of 1348, known as the Black Death, and subsequent French sea raids during the 15th Century.

Beyond a swing gate, bear half right, dropping down into the Cuckmere valley once more with the farm buildings at Foxhole nestling down in a valley to your left. The barn up the hill above the farm provides overnight camping facilities for South Downs Way walkers.

At the bottom **(2**, go forward on a hard track, after a few yards forking left. Go through a bridle gate and up steps. Ignoring a stile, follow a fence, right, steadily up and out to the cliff edge on the summit of the first of the Seven Sisters. Turn left and follow the undulating, somewhat eroded cliff path over three more of the Seven Sister and up to the

Exceat Farm and The Cuckmere River.

top of a fourth. On the summit of the third sister you will enter the National Trust area of Crowlink and on the top of the fourth sister you will come to a well placed seat and a memorial sarsen stone (3).

The stone commemorates the purchase of the Crowlink estate during the 1920s for the public benefit, at a time when the whole area was threatened by housing development. It is now in the safe hands of the National Trust.

At the memorial stone, turn squarely left away from the sea and follow a worn path along a ridge. Beyond a gate, maintain direction across open downland, aiming for a small group of stunted trees on the near skyline. Pass to the right of these trees and head for a gate which now comes into sight. Once through this gate, go almost directly ahead, aiming just to the right of a more substantial planted tree clump. Pass to the right of this clump, dropping downhill with a fence on your left.

When you come to a point where two walls meet, go over steps in the right hand wall and follow this wall, now on your left, downhill. From the field corner a concrete path with handrail takes you down into East Dean, Turn left along a lane (Went Way). Join Upper Street and go forward along the left hand edge of the village green (4).

The Tiger Inn , on the other side of the green, is a popular watering hole, which can get very crowded in Summer, though there is plenty of room for patrons to spill out on to the green when the weather is dry and warm.

Friston Church.

37

The Cliff Path along The Seven Sisters, Belle Tout in Background.

After a few more yards, where the road bends to the right, go ahead along the concrete access drive to the Farrar Hall. Beyond a gate, maintain the same direction, climbing steadily up a long grassy slope. At the top, walk out through Friston churchyard to join an access drive with Friston Pond in front of you.

The church is mainly of Norman origin with additions from the 13th to 15th Centuries. Inside are several monuments to the Selwyn family who lived in Friston Place, passed later on the walk. The church and a handful of houses which make up the original village, now vastly extended, are grouped near the attractive village pond, unusually high for a downland village, at 350 feet above sea level.

*Turn right out to the A259 **(5)**. Cross the main road, go forward across the middle of a triangle of grass, over a slip road and ahead over steps in a wall, signed as a public footpath to Snap Hill. On the other side of the wall, fork right on a clear woodland path which drops down, skirting to the left of a covered reservoir. Leave the wood and descend across the middle of a large field with Friston Forest spread out ahead and to your left.*

Cross a drive where gates and steps are provided and continue down across another field. Go through a gate in a flint wall and turn left along a bridleway which runs parallel and to the right of an access drive. After about 250 yards, turn left along a crossing track which, after a few yards, joins and follows a roughly metalled access drive.

Ignoring a right fork, go ahead, soon passing to the left of Friston Pumping Station. Beyond a house on the right, the track dwindles to a path which begins to climb up into Friston Forest. Shortly, at a T- junction (6), turn right and follow a wide track through planted, maturing beech woodland, ignoring the first left fork up through the woods to your left.

Friston Forest covers almost 2000 acres. Tree planting began in 1926 and the area is now maturing into a broadleaved forest, mainly beech.

After about 350 yards, at a way post, fork left uphill. Go over a crossing track and continue out to the A259 (7). Cross the road, go through a gate opposite and follow an unfenced access drive which hairpins down to reach an attractive barn complex.

The New Barn complex was recently threatened with development into a residential educational centre with additional building and attendant lighting and car parking etc. After strong objections from conservationists, including the Society of Sussex Downsmen, the planning application was turned down. It is now hoped that New Barn can be restored for agricultural use, surely the only acceptable purpose for buildings in this lovely secluded valley.

Pass to the right of New Barn and down along the floor of New Barn Bottom, soon on a grassy track. About 150 yards past a cottage, go ahead with a fence on your left (not through the first gate) which you can now follow for about three quarters of a mile. At Foxhole Farm (8), just past a large barn on your left you will come to a stile in this fence. Don't cross it. Instead, fork right with your back to the stile and follow a path, between banks at first, then with a low bank on the right only, over the low shoulder of a hill, crossing your outgoing route, and back to the start which is soon in sight.

Walk 8
ALFRISTON, LULLINGTON HEATH AND LITLINGTON

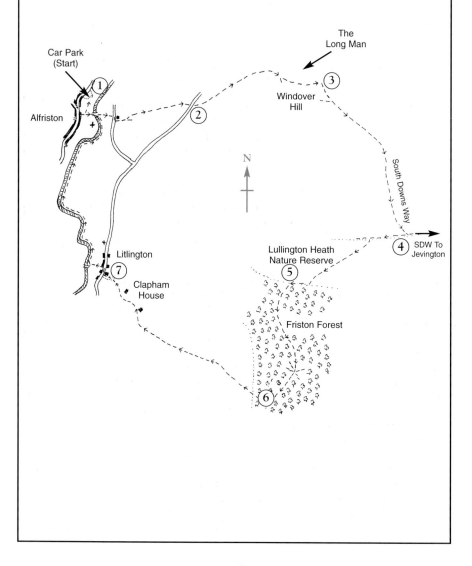

Car Park (Start)

The Long Man

Alfriston

Windover Hill

N

South Downs Way

SDW To Jevington

Lullington Heath Nature Reserve

Litlington

Clapham House

Friston Forest

Walk 8
ALFRISTON, LULLINGTON HEATH
AND LITLINGTON

Distance:	7 miles.
Route:	Alfriston - Windover Hill - top of Jevington Holt - Lullington Heath Nature Reserve - Friston Forest - Litlington - Alfriston.
Map:	OS Explorer 123: South Downs Way - Newhaven to Eastbourne.
Start/Parking:	In the Willows long stay car park at the northern edge of the village of Alfriston (GR 521032).
Public Transport:	Occasional weekday bus service from Eastbourne and Lewes. At weekends during the summer months, the Cuckmere Valley Ramblerbus offers an hourly bus service from Berwick Station to Alfriston and various other points in the Cuckmere Valley.
Conditions:	Good walking along chalk and flint or grassy tracks. One steady climb on to the Downs at the start, otherwise gently undulating with no steep gradients.
Refreshments:	Pubs and tea rooms at Alfriston. Plough and Harrow pub and tea room at Litlington.

Within its fairly modest seven mile length, this walk embraces a remarkable variety of features. Starting across high open chalk downland, it crosses the Lullington Heath nature reserve where alkaline and acid soils combine to provide an important habitat, unique in the area. After passing through a corner of the broad leaved woodland of Friston Forest, the walk crosses more undulating downland to Litlington and finishes with a short stroll beside the Cuckmere River.

Before or after the walk, allow time to explore the village of Alfriston. In the small village square stands a rather battered medieval market-cross, one of the only remaining examples in Sussex. Along the village street is the 15th century Star Inn, previously a hostel for pilgrims on their way to the shrine of St Richard in Chichester. On the other side of the street stands the George Inn which dates from about the same time. Another pub, favoured by walkers, once the Market Cross, is now Ye Olde Smugglers Inn, and reminds us that, in the 18th Century the village was a centre of the smuggling industry, within easy reach of a convenient landing place for contraband goods at Cuckmere Haven. The church, which has acquired the sobriquet 'Cathedral of the Downs' is, indeed, an imposing structure, standing a little apart from the village on a low mound overlooking the village green and the Cuckmere River.

THE WALK

From the car park **(1)** walk into the centre of Alfriston. Just past the George Inn on the left, turn left along a narrow path which takes you down past the village green, over the Cuckmere River and on to join a lane opposite a restored barn, Plonk Barn on the map, but now renamed as Great Meadow Barn. Turn right and, after 10 yards, go left along a narrow path, signposted to Lullington and Jevington.

After about 150 yards, turn left with the South Downs Way on a path which climbs obliquely up across two fields where it is usually marked and trodden out through any growing crop. Join a track and turn right for a few yards out to a lane **(2)**.

Cross the road and follow a track, opposite, which climbs steadily up on to the shoulder of Windover Hill, passing to the right of a prominent covered reservoir on the skyline. Go through a gate and, after 150 yards, where the main track veers right round the right shoulder of the hill, you should go directly ahead. Keep a fence on your left, passing above the chalk figure of the Long Man of Wilmington. As you approach the highest point **(3)**, ignore a bridle gate in front of you and instead, follow the fence round to the right and then left. Now head out across a fine open downland ridge, walking parallel to a line of gorse

Alfriston High Street.

42

Litlington.

Approaching Alfriston.

Alfriston Church and Village.

on your left and rejoining the South Downs Way, which is undefined except for a series of wooden wayposts.

Eventually the South Downs Way passes through gates and continues between hedges. At a broad crossing track (4), turn sharply back to the right. Follow the track, passing to the right of a notice at the start of Lullington Heath Nature Reserve. Keep to the track as it passes along the right edge of the reserve until, after about 250 yards you can fork left through a swing gate at the start of a numbered nature trail.

Lullington Heath National Nature Reserve was established in 1955, mainly because of the acid soil which lies on top of the chalk in part of the 150 acre site, allowing a rare combination of acid and alkaline loving plants to grow together. To help check the scrub which would otherwise take over the area, the land is grazed by an assortment of unusual animals which can cope with this environment. You may spot New Forest ponies, Welsh Beulah sheep or Bagot's Goats.

Follow a path through the reserve until, at a crossing ride at the edge of Friston Forest you can turn right. At the bottom of a dip (5), turn left on a wide grassy track through Friston Forest, signposted to Charleston Bottom. At a meeting of six ways, go half right, still on a wide ride along the valley floor. After about 300 yards, at a waypost in the middle of the ride (6), fork right, signposted to Litlington. Leave the forest through a bridle gate and continue on a track which takes an undulating downland route for over a mile before bringing you down to join a lane at Litlington.

Turn right. A few yards past the Plough and Harrow pub (7), go left along a narrow enclosed path which takes you down to the Cuckmere River. Turn right along the near side river bank and follow it for a mile, before turning left over the bridge at Alfriston. Just past the bridge, a signed path to the right provides a direct route back to the car park.

Walk 9
GLYNDE, SAXON CROSS AND MOUNT CABURN

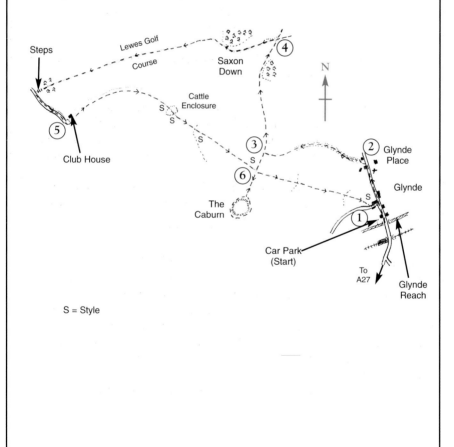

Steps

Lewes Golf Course

Saxon Down

Cattle Enclosure

Club House

The Caburn

Glynde Place

Glynde

Car Park (Start)

To A27

Glynde Reach

N

S = Style

Walk 9
GLYNDE, SAXON CROSS AND MOUNT CABURN

Distance:	6 ¹/₄ miles.
Route:	Glynde - Saxon Down - Saxon Cross - Cliffe Hill - Oxteddle Bottom - The Caburn - Glynde.
Map:	OS Explorer 122: South Downs Way - Steyning to Newhaven.
Start/Parking:	The village of Glynde, accessible from the A27 about three miles east of Lewes. Park in the newly refurbished car park, immediately to the north of Glynde railway station. (GR 458088).
Public Transport:	Regular train service to Glynde Station from Lewes or Eastbourne.
Conditions:	One steady climb at the start, then easy walking over high open downland and across Lewes Golf Course. The return route involves a descent into a quiet downland valley and another long climb up to Mount Caburn.
Refreshments:	Trevor Arms pub at Glynde, within a few yards of the start. Pubs aplenty in Lewes, half a mile off the route.

Separated from the main ridge of the downs by the Glynde valley, the isolated outcrop of chalk hills between Glynde and Lewes, rising to almost 500 feet at the summit of Mount Caburn, offer some of the very best downland walking. This was not always so. A walk similar to this one was included in an early version of 'On Foot in East Sussex' but had to be deleted from later editions because of fence obstructions, extensive ploughing and the unmarked state of some of the paths. Waymarking of the path across Lewes Golf Course has greatly improved matters. As a bonus, Environmentally Sensitive Area designation means that much of the area has been allowed, at least for the time being, to revert to pasture.

THE WALK

From the entrance to the car park *(1)* turn left and walk along the whole length of the main street, passing the village blacksmith's forge, the church and the entrance to Glynde Place, all on the right.

The church, in Palladian style, was designed and constructed, using Portland Stone, in 1763. Glynde Place is an Elizabethan house, built partly using local flint. Since the early 19th Century it has been the home of the Hampden family and is open to the public during the summer months on Wednesday, Thursday and Sunday afternoons from 2 to 5.

About 100 yards past Glynde Place, turn left through a gateway (2) and immediately right, signposted as a licensed footpath to Mount Caburn. Follow this track steadily uphill on to the downs.

A well placed memorial seat offers an excuse for a breather as well as a fine view across the Ouse valley towards the main downland ridge between Kingston Hill and Firle Beacon.

Where the path levels out a junction of tracks (3), turn right to follow a path across high open downland. Beyond a stile, go ahead, descending into a shallow dip before skirting along the rim of a wooded combe, dropping away to your right.

Shortly you should be able to catch a glimpse of the ugly square top of the new Glyndebourne Opera House protruding from the trees in the valley to your right. The original Elizabethan mansion is largely hidden from view.

On reaching another stile beside a gate (4), turn sharply back to the left and climb back up on to high ground with a fence on your right at first. Keep with the main track as it bears right above another wooded combe on the northern flank of Saxon Down. Beyond a stile the path continues in a straight line along the hillside with a deep valley (Bible Bottom) dropping away to your left and a fence about 50 yards to your right. Go straight ahead across the golf course where the right of way is marked by a series of wooden way posts and yellow arrows which should be followed with care. As you reach each post, the next one should be in sight. Beyond the playing area a path goes ahead, dropping steeply down through trees to join a metalled road.

If in need of refreshment, turn right down the hill into Lewes. Otherwise, turn left and follow this private access road to Lewes Golf Course, climbing again. A path on top of the bank to your right offers a spectacular view over the River Ouse and Lewes. Skirt to the right of the golf club car park (5) and follow a grassy path which takes a level course along the hill side before dropping obliquely down through scattered scrub. At a stile, fork right, dropping diagonally down across the middle of a field. At the bottom, cross a stile and pass through an often muddy cattle feeding area and carry on along the floor of a dry valley (Oxteddle Bottom). Beyond a stile, follow a grassy strip which climbs steadily up, diverging at about 20 degrees from the fence on your right.

At the top you will come to a newish stile (6). From here, your path back to Glynde goes straight ahead but you should be sure not to omit the short detour to the right, up to the summit of Mount Caburn.

At 491 feet, Caburn is the highest point on the walk, commanding exceptional views across the Ouse valley. The summit is crowned by an Iron Age fort dating from about 500 BC, with a double rampart and ditch. The whole area is designated as a National Nature Reserve on which you may wander freely. It provides a protected haven for a rich variety of downland flowers.

Follow the clear well trodden path down a broad ridge to Glynde. At a lane, turn left past the village shop and right back to the start.

The path up to Saxon Down.

Walk 10
FIRLE, ALCISTON AND BERWICK

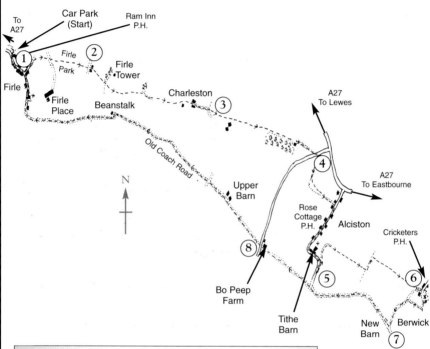

Alciston Church and Medieval Dovecote.

Walk 10
FIRLE, ALCISTON AND BERWICK

Distance:	8 miles.
Route:	Firle - Charleston Farm - Alciston - Berwick - Old Coach Road - Firle.
Map:	OS Explorer 123: South Downs Way - Newhaven to Eastbourne.
Start/Parking:	At the village of Firle, signposted from the A27 Lewes-to-Eastbourne road about four miles east of Lewes. Follow the signs to Firle Village. The car park is on the northern edge of the village at GR 468074.
Public Transport:	Occasional weekday bus from Lewes (five services daily).
Conditions:	Field paths and tracks along the foot of the Downs. No significant hills. The return route from Berwick is likely to be muddy underfoot in places.
Refreshments:	Ram Inn at Firle, Rose Cottage Inn at Alciston and the Cricketers at Berwick.

This circuit, unique among the walks in this collection, stays off the Downs to link three of the delightful villages situated at the foot of the northern escarpment. These settlements were first established to benefit from the never failing supply of water which bubbles out from under the chalk hills.

The walk starts at Firle (West Firle on maps though there is now no East Firle and the 'West' was officially dropped some years ago). It then visits Charleston and passes through Alciston to reach Berwick. Your return route follows part of the Old Coach Road, in use until 1812 when the present road to Eastbourne was constructed. It may be muddy in places but you are compensated by ever changing views of the escarpment rising to Firle Beacon, visited on Walk 15.

THE WALK

From the far end of the car park *(1)* go through a white gate and turn right along a track out to the village street near the Ram Inn. Turn left and follow the lane until you can go left along an unmade track which starts beside the post office/stores. Once out into Firle Park, diverge slightly to the right of the track to follow a route across the park, marked by a series of wayposts with yellow arrows and crossing the main drive to Firle Place.

Firle Place is now in view to your right. The original house was built for Sir John Gage, Lord Chamberlain to Henry VIII, during the 15th Century. The remaining fragments of the Tudor building are now encased by the present mansion, the work of the first Viscount Gage, who erected the present Georgian style north-east front in around 1750. The house is notable for an exceptional collection of paintings, furniture and porcelain. It is open from May to September on Sundays, Wednesdays and Thursdays from 2 to 5.

On the other side of the park *(2)* go through a bridle gate, cross a drive and go ahead between two cottages. Pass through an iron gate and follow a trodden path up across a field. At the top of a low rise go through a belt of woodland and ahead across three more fields.

Up the hill to your left is Firle Tower. Its origins are uncertain but it was used as a gamekeeper's cottage and also as a signalling tower from which messages could be sent to the nearby Plashett Estate, also in the ownership of the Gage family.

In the far corner of the third field, go left through a bridle gate and, after a few yards, right, walking parallel to a hedge and ditch on your right. Beyond the end of the field, a farm track continues past a farm to Charleston.

Charleston Farm House was the home of Vanessa Bell and Duncan Grant, artists at the centre of the so called Bloomsbury Group of writers, artists and intellectuals, including Virginia Woolf, E M Forster and Lytton Strachey. When Duncan Grant died in 1978, the Charleston Trust was formed to restore and preserve the house. It is now open to the public during the summer months from Wednesday to Sunday between 2 and 6.

Follow the access drive from Charleston. At a T-junction with another drive *(3)*, go directly ahead through a gap and follow power lines along a headland track. The track continues, a bit vague in places, in the same direction, soon passing to the left of Tilton Wood and a small pottery. An access drive takes you out to a lane.

Turn left and, after 30 yards *(4)* go right over a stile and walk downhill along a left field edge with a wide sweep of the downs escarpment directly ahead. In the field corner cross two stiles and bear half left, obliquely up a slope. In the far field corner you have a choice of stiles. Go over the one on the left and forward along a left field edge to join the village street at Alciston.

Turn right, soon passing the Rose Cottage pub on your right. Carry on past the church on your left and where the lane bends left, the tithe barn, also on the left.

The grouping of 13th Century church, 14th Century tithe barn and home farm, incorporating the remains of a medieval dovecote, is a delight.

Follow the lane as it bears left by the Tithe Barn and then right to head towards the Downs. After another 100 yards (5), go left through a wide gap and double back along a left field edge. In the field corner, turn right within the same field, keeping the hedge on your left, with the spire of Berwick Church directly ahead. In the next field corner go through a gap and left, still keeping a hedge on your left. After 130 yards, turn right and head for Berwick once more, now on a grassy strip between two fields. A rutted track and then a concrete farm access drive take you out to the lane at Berwick (6).

The Cricketers Inn is now a short distance along the lane to the left but, to continue the walk, go through a wide gap opposite. Now bear half right over a stile and along the right edge of a meadow with a house and garden and then a high flint wall on your right. Enter Berwick churchyard through a wicket gate.

Berwick church with its fine shingled spire, is notable for a number of modern murals, painted by Duncan Grant, Vanessa Bell and Quentin Bell depicting biblical scenes in modern settings.

Leave the churchyard down steps to the right of the church entrance and turn left along a path. Once out into the open at a fine viewpoint, turn right along a wide track. After about 300 yards, at a T-junction with another farm track turn left and head for the Downs. After another 380 yards (7), at a T-junction, turn right.

You are now on the Old Coach Road, waymarked in red, indicating that the path is still classified as a byway open to vehicular traffic as well as walkers and riders. A few yards along the track, on the left is New Barn a typical cluster of barn, cattle shelter and flint walled compound, sheltered by trees, a frequent and characteristic feature of the East Sussex Downs.

The Old Coach Road now unwinds on a gently undulating route along the foot of the Downs for over three miles back to Firle. After two thirds of a mile, where the track from Alciston joins from the right, go straight ahead, and after another half a mile, at Bo-peep Farm (8), cross the Firle Bostal road. Ignore another crossing track and after a further mile or so you will come to Beanstalk a house with lancet windows, once a Coaching Inn at a time when there were four pubs in the Firle area.

Go left and right with the main track, muddy along this section though, like other walkers before you, you may be able to escape into the field to the left to avoid the worst of the mud. Ignore tracks to right and left, continuing with the flint wall surrounding Firle Park on your right. The track finally veers right and takes you past a farm and into Firle village.

Access to the Church of St Peter is on the right. The Tower and Nave date from the 13th Century. Inside are some exceptional brasses and a number of Gage family tombs. Look out also for a window, designed by John Piper and installed in 1985 in memory of the Sixth Viscount Gage.

Follow the village street back to the Ram Inn and the start.

Walk 11
SOUTHEASE AND RODMELL

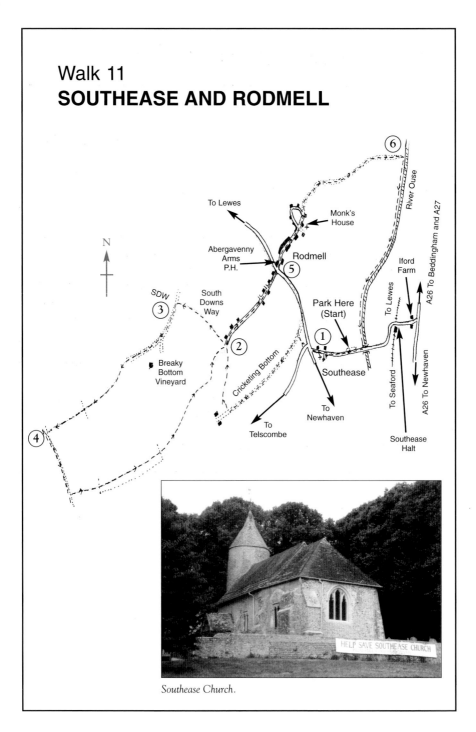

Southease Church.

Walk 11
SOUTHEASE AND RODMELL

Distance:	7¹/₂ miles.
Route:	Southease - South Downs Way - Mill Hill - Highdole Hill - Mill Hill - Rodmell - River Ouse - Southease.
Map:	OS Explorer 122: South Downs Way - Steyning to Newhaven.
Start/Parking:	Roadside parking just east of Southease Bridge. From the Newhaven-to Lewes road, turn east along the No Through Road to Southease. Beyond the village there are various places to park on the grass verge (GR 427053). NB there is no vehicular access across the railway at Southease Halt, so do not approach the start from the A26.
Public Transport:	Train from Brighton or Lewes to Southease Station.
Conditions:	All on firm downland tracks or across open grass downland; raised river bank on final section.
Refreshments:	Abergavenny Arms pub at Rodmell.

The two unspoilt villages of Southease and Rodmell provide the focus of this walk. The full circuit of just over seven miles is in the form of a figure-of-eight, allowing flexibility for anyone looking for a shorter walk. The two sections can be enjoyed separately or combined to provide a pleasantly contrasted experience of gentle rolling downland followed by open river valley.

THE WALK

From wherever you managed to park walk back along the road into Southease Village **(1)**.

Allow time to look into the tiny flint church with its striking round tower, one of three such church towers in Sussex, all in the Ouse valley. The other two are at Piddinghoe and Lewes and the three churches form a straight line, a fact of significance to believers in ley lines. Another theory is that they were built to function as beacon towers when the river was navigable. The church incorporates a Norman nave with 14th century additions and some 13th century paintings uncovered in 1935.

At the Newhaven-to Lewes road, turn right. After a few yards, turn into the cul-de-sac to Telscombe on the left, and immediately turn right through a bridle gate, signposted as the South Downs Way. This is a new section of this long distance route, which you will be following for a little over a mile. Cross a grassy mound and bear half right to enter a path which winds down through scrub to join a farm track where you should turn left.

Follow this gravel track along the floor of a peaceful downland valley (Cricketing Bottom). After a little over half a mile, about 100 yards short of farm buildings, turn right with the South Downs Way which follows a rutted track for 100 yards or so before bearing right through a bridle gate to climb gently up a downland spur. At the top **(2)** *cross the end of the access road to a house called Mill Hill on your left and go ahead on a narrow shady path between fence and hedge. The path soon opens out with fine views across the Ouse valley to Lewes and the downland outlier of Mount Caburn.*

After another 600 yards or so, at a concrete crossing track **(3)**, *turn left, parting company with the South Downs Way. Where the track divides, fork right. This chalk*

and flint track drops down into a valley with the tiny vineyard of Breaky Bottom nestling down in a hollow to your left. From the bottom of the hill go ahead on a rough track between fences and then with a fence on your right only which soon climbs gently, to a stile and then in the same direction up across open downland. At the top a view

Breaky Bottom Vineyard.

of the sea opens out ahead, glimpsed through a gap in the Downs at Rottingdean with the suburban sprawl of Saltdean also prominent.

Go through a gate (4) and turn left along a clear track across the high ground of Highdole Hill. After about 550 yards turn left through a weighted bridle gate where a

Rodmell.

yellow arrow indicates the start of a footpath. Head out across open downland, veering very slightly right and aiming for another bridle gate. Once through this gate your route now contours along the open hill side with a line of gorse away to your left at first, converging eventually on a fence to your right. Go through another gate in the far right corner of this long field and veer slightly left down a descending grassy ridge. At the bottom go left and right with a path which climbs along the left edge of pasture up to the top of Mill Hill, back at point 2.

Cross your outgoing route and follow the access road down to the foot of the Downs. Cross the Newhaven-to-Lewes road by the Abergavenny Arms (5) and follow the No Though Road, opposite, down through Rodmell village.

Although expanded in recent years with the addition of a number of new houses, Rodmell still manages to retain much of its old world charm and beauty. The flint walls which are a feature of the village have been largely retained and there are a number of old cottages. Access to the carefully restored Norman church is on the right via the village school yard. Just past the church is Monk's House, once the home of Virginia and Leonard Woolf. It is now looked after by the National Trust and is open on Wednesdays and Saturdays from April to October between 2 p.m. and 5.30 p.m..

About 100 yards past Monk's House fork right along a gravel track which leads out on to the Brooks, an area of extensive drained water meadows. It takes you, after a little over half a mile out to reach the River Ouse (6). Turn right and follow the raised river bank down stream for about a mile back to Southease Swing Bridge which still retains its original wooden supports. Turn right along the road back to the point from which you started.

Walk 12
STANMER, DITCHLING BEACON AND THE SOUTH DOWNS WAY

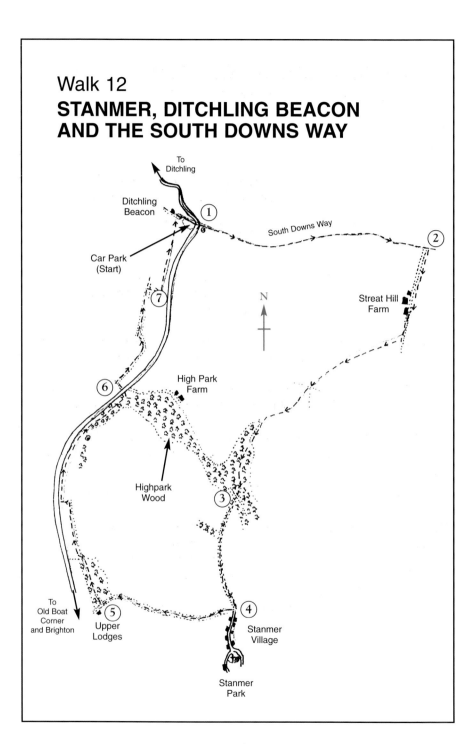

Walk 12
STANMER, DITCHLING BEACON
AND THE SOUTH DOWNS WAY

Distance:	6¹/₂ miles.
Route:	Ditchling Beacon - Streat Hill - Stanmer Village - Upper Lodges - Highpark Corner - Ditchling Beacon.
Map:	OS Explorer 122: South Downs Way - Steyning to Newhaven.
Start/Parking:	You can start the walk either from the National Trust car park at Ditchling Beacon (GR 332130) or from Stanmer Park, joining the walk at point 4.
Public Transport:	Regular bus service from Brighton to Sussex University, about half a mile from point 4 through Stanmer Park.
Conditions:	Excellent, along good paths or farm tracks. One short section of tarmac but with restricted vehicular access.
Refreshments:	Tea shop, also serving breakfasts and light lunches, attached to the village store at Stanmer, a few yards off the route from point 4.

This is a variant of a popular circuit for local people, linking Stanmer Park on the northern edge of Brighton with the highest point on the eastern Downs at Ditchling Beacon, just over 800 feet above sea level. In spite of the considerable climb, the gradients are always gentle and the 'going' good along firm well drained paths and tracks. The walk description starts and finishes at Ditchling Beacon but Stanmer Park provides an equally convenient starting point, joining the walk at point 4.

THE WALK

From the car park **(1)**, cross the Ditchling Beacon road and, leaving a restored dewpond on your right, start the walk by heading eastwards along the South Downs Way. Follow this track along the summit of the escarpment. For most of the way, your route uses a fine open route between widely spaced fences, with glorious views northwards across the Weald.

After a little over a mile **(2)**, go across another road coming up from the foot of the Downs. After 10 yards, turn right along a headland track which runs parallel to an access road behind the hedge to your right. Just after passing the buildings of Streathill Farm on your right, turn right over a stile and bear left along a track which keeps to the left of an open sided barn and continues southwards along a left field edge.

After about 250 yards, at a waypost, veer half right across the middle of a large field, normally down to arable, though there should be a marked path across any growing

The path of Streat Hill.

crop. On the far side of the field go over a stile and maintain direction across a field corner to a bridle gate. A grassy track now drops obliquely down the hillside into a quiet downland valley before winding along the valley floor.

The track skirts to the left of a block of woodland before entering the wood to climb gently. At a meeting of four ways **(3)** go straight ahead on a clear track which takes you down into the next valley. At the edge of the village of Stanmer **(4)**, just past a small pond on the right, our walk continues along a bridleway.

Allow time if possible to walk on through the village and into Stanmer Park. The Village Store with attached tea room is on the left. The church was rebuilt in 1838 and contains a marble memorial to Sir John Pelham. Next to the church is the 250 ft well, first bored in the 16th century. Until 1870, the water was raised by means of a donkey wheel, 13 ft in diameter which can still be glimpsed through a murky glass panel in the door of the well house. Stroll on past the church and village pond for a good view of Stanmer House, dating from 1725 and

Stanmer House.

for many years the seat of the Pelham family.

*Reverse your steps and continue the walk from point **4**, through a gate, locked to restrict vehicular use, and steadily up along the metalled lane to Upper Lodges. About 80 yards short of a white walled cottage **(5)** turn right, and immediately, keep along the main track, ignoring a right fork. Similarly, ignore another track leading out into a field on your left. Head north along a substantial woodland track, still gradually gaining height.*

Leave the wood over a stile, go half left to a second stile and resume your previous direction along the right edge of an area of rough pasture. When in line with overhead power lines, turn left towards the Ditchling Beacon road where there is a stile. **Don't** *cross this stile, instead turn right and walk along the left field edge, parallel to the road.*

Soon after passing a dew pond on your right, go over a stile and follow a woodland path northwards, still parallel to the road but well screened from it by trees. Where the path divides, fork left and shortly, cross the road and go through the bridle gate, opposite **(6)**. *Keep to the left edge of the first field, In the field corner, go through a weighted*

Ditchling Beacon from Bottal Hill.

gate and turn right beside a fence, soon curving round the head of a downland combe. In the next field corner turn right through a gate and follow a wide fenced track uphill.

Where the track begins to level out, turn right through a bridle gate and along another, unfenced, track. About 100 yards short of the road **(7)**, turn left and head northwards along a grassy strip.

From point 7, looking eastwards along the line of the Downs, you can pick out the distinctive shapes of Mount Caburn and Firle Beacon, facing each other across the valley, and nearer and a little to the right, the profile of Kingston Hill.

A ten minute walk brings you back up to the summit of Ditchling Beacon. Beyond a bridle gate the trig point is a few yards to the left, the car park a similar distance to the right.

Walk 13
WILLINGDON HILL, EAST DEAN AND BELLE TOUT

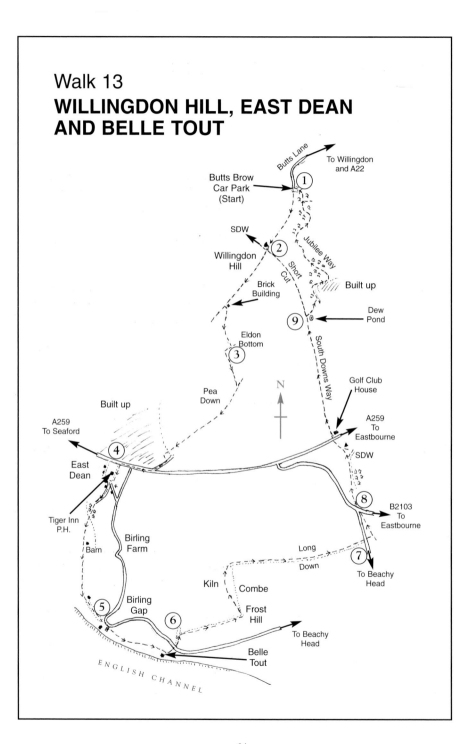

Walk 13
WILLINGDON HILL, EAST DEAN AND BELLE TOUT

Distance:	11 miles.
Route:	Butts Brow Car Park - Willingdon Hill - Pea Down -East Dean - Birling Gap - Belle Tout - Long Down - South Downs Way - Jubilee Way - Butts Brow Car Park.
Map:	OS Explorer 123: South Downs Way - Newhaven to Eastbourne.
Start/Parking:	From the A22 at Willingdon, if travelling north, turn left along Church Street or, if travelling south, turn right along Cooper's Hill, continuing through Willingdon and up Butts Lane on to the top of the Downs. Park in the large car park and picnic area where the lane ends (GR 580017),
Public Transport:	Regular bus service along the coast road to East Dean, allowing you to join the walk at point 4.
Conditions:	Excellent walking, mostly across dry open downland. Quite strenuous with a number of ups and downs as the walk cuts across the grain of the land.
Refreshments:	Tiger Inn at East Dean, pub and coffee shop at Birling Gap.

Much of this walk is within the 4000 acres of Eastbourne Heritage Downland. Sensitive management has ensured that the area has not been marred by the intensive ploughing and cultivation found elsewhere in the Downs. For much of the route you can enjoy ideal downland walking with short cropped sheep pasture beneath your feet and unrestricted by fences. Most of the eastern escarpment south of Willingdon Hill is a public open access area on which you can wander freely.

The recently published Definitive Map of rights of way on the Eastbourne downland includes one or two excellent paths not available to compilers of earlier editions of 'On Foot'. Two of these paths, through Eldon Bottom and up the ridge of Frost Hill, are incorporated into this circuit.

THE WALK

From the car park **(1)** follow a bridleway signposted to Friston and Beachy Head on both a wooden post and a carved stone marker, made from stone salvaged from an Eastbourne bank, bombed out during World War II. Follow a level route along the upper hillside, passing about 100 yards to the right of a radio mast. You have a choice of parallel tracks all within a public open access area. A view soon opens up to the left across Eastbourne.

Climb gently up on to Willingdon Hill. Walk past the trig point on the summit **(2)**, cross the South Downs Way, go through a bridle gate and ahead along a wide ridge with the village of Jevington in view, nestling down in the valley to your right. After a little over half a mile, just short of a rather ugly modern brick shed, turn left over a stile and follow a delightful grassy path which veers right and drops down into a dry downland valley (Eldon Bottom).

Cross the valley floor to a stile beside a gate **(3)** and continue with a fence, right, for a short distance before veering left obliquely up the side of the hill, aiming for a line of gorse on the skyline. Bear right at the top leaving the gorse on your left. A path continues on a straight course down the ridge of Pea Down. At the bottom go over two stiles at the edge of the built up area and follow an enclosed path between gardens. Where it divides, keep left. At an estate road go forward to a T-junction with another access drive and turn right to follow it out to the A259. Bear right and walk down into East Dean.

When opposite the start of Michel Dene Road to the right **(4)**, turn left between staggered railings and follow a path through to the Tiger Inn and the village green.

The old village of East Dean centred round the Tiger Inn and the green is an idyllic spot, particularly out of season. The nearby Norman church is worth the short detour.

From the pub go ahead across the green, turn left along Upper Street and immediately fork right along a No Through Road, Went Way. Where this road ends, go through a gate from which a clear track climbs obliquely up through woodland and out on to the open National Trust area of Crowlink. Now aim for the sea passing to the right of a barn on the skyline and dropping down to a bridle gate. Go forward to a second bridle gate and on down to Birling Gap **(5)**.

Birling Gap is now in the hands of the National Trust and has been considerably tidied up in recent years. A mobile set of steps allow access to the beach and there is a conveniently placed pub and coffee shop, open throughout the year.

On the other side of the gap climb steps and up on to the cliffs. Follow the cliff path as far as the Belle Tout lighthouse.

Belle Tout lighthouse was built within a historic earthwork in 1831, but superseded in 1902 by the present Beachy Head Light at the foot of the cliffs. Recent cliff falls left Belle Tout precariously placed on the cliff edge. In 1999, with

Path down into Eldon Bottom.

East Dean, The Village Green.

Birling Gap and The Seven Sisters.

Belle Tout, before the move.

collapse into the sea imminent, the whole building was raised on jacks and moved bodily inland, allowing it a new lease of life.

Pass the lighthouse on the landward side and, when opposite the far end of the lighthouse enclosure, turn left and pick your way with care down the steep scrub covered slope where there is a path of sorts. At the bottom cross the coast road and follow the concrete drive to Cornish Farm

After about 100 yards (6), turn right, signposted to Eastbourne, and follow a fence, left, up on to Frost Hill. After almost two thirds of a mile, in the field corner, turn left through a bridle gate and follow a grassy bridleway over a ridge, down into Kiln Combe and up again with a fence on your right. At the top of the slope go through a bridle gate and turn right along the gradually rising ridge of Long Down for more than a mile.

Cross the Beachy Head road (7) and follow the waymarked bridleway opposite out across open downland where the view over Eastbourne reappears with the coast beyond stretching into the distance as far as the cliffs at Fairlight on the other side of Hastings. At a sign, turn left, and follow a clear path. Cross the B2103 opposite its junction with the Beachy Head Road (8) and continue along a signed bridleway which soon skirts above a wooded combe

After a quarter of a mile, where the main track veers right, you should bear left up to a seat on the skyline. Pass to the left of a dew pond and a trig point and continue on a wide grassy path along the escarpment, part of the South Downs Way.

Cross the A259 to the left of a golf club house, and follow a clear track through the golf course. Beyond the playing area you can avoid the hard track by walking on a parallel grass track to the right, within the Eastbourne Downland open access area. For the shortest and easiest way back to Butts Brow, follow the South Downs Way as far as the summit of Willingdon Hill, and turn right to retrace your outgoing route.

For a most attractive alternative, much of it within woodland in complete contrast to the rest of the walk, just past a dew pond (9), turn right and follow a waymarked bridleway down through scrub. Towards the bottom, turn left on a crossing path, part of the Jubilee Way, marked with a crown logo.

The Jubilee Way is a waymarked route, established by Eastbourne Borough Council. It follows the 300 foot contour for about five miles along the lower slope of the eastern downs escarpment from Butts Lane to the sea at Holywell.

Follow the Jubilee Way for two thirds of a mile on path which contours behind an estate and to the left of a golf course. On reaching a junction of paths take the second of two paths to the right, signed with a green arrow. Follow the green arrowed track which soon climbs steadily round a wooded combe. Towards the top, fork left, still with a green arrow to guide you. After a few yards you will be back at the Butts Brow picnic area and car park.

Walk 14
WILMINGTON, JEVINGTON, FRISTON FOREST AND THE CUCKMERE VALLEY

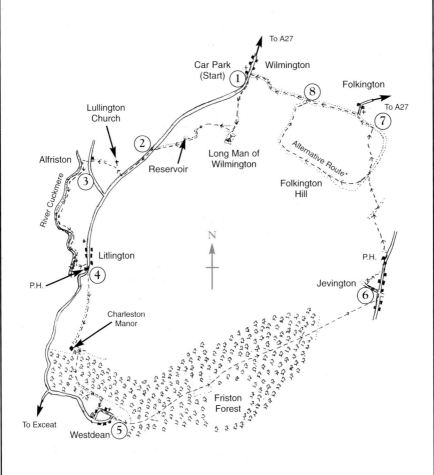

*Available until
September 2002

Walk 14
WILMINGTON, JEVINGTON, FRISTON FOREST AND THE CUCKMERE VALLEY

Distance:	10 miles.
Route:	Wilmington- Long Man - Lullington Church -Alfriston - Litlington - Westdean - Friston Forest - Jevington - Folkington - Wilmington.
Map:	OS Explorer 123: South Downs Way - Newhaven to Eastbourne.
Start/Parking:	The village of Wilmington, to the south of the A27 Lewes-to-Eastbourne road. The car park is at the far (southern) end of the village street, beyond the church and Wilmington Priory (GR 544041).
Public Transport:	Bus service from Eastbourne to Wilmington cross roads (five services daily in each direction - Monday to Saturday only).
Conditions:	Mostly along chalk and flint tracks and forest rides plus short sections along a raised riverbank and across open downland. Several hills, none particularly severe.
Refreshments:	Pubs at Wilmington, Alfriston, Litlington and Jevington. Tea rooms at Alfriston and Litlington.

This is a walk of contrasts, as rich and varied as any on the South Downs. It embraces open grass downland, riverbank and the sheltered woodland of Friston Forest. It visits five unspoilt villages and passes close to no less than seven downland churches, as well as offering a close look at the well-known chalk figure of the Long Man of Wilmington.

THE WALK

Set out along a signposted path to the Long Man, which starts opposite the car park entrance **(1)***. On reaching the foot of the hill figure, turn right on a path which climbs round the shoulder of Windover Hill. Go straight over a crossing track. On reaching a fence, turn left beside it and, after 30 yards go right through a gate. Now follow a sunken track which passes to the left of a covered reservoir and drops down towards the Cuckmere valley. Alfriston is soon directly ahead backed by a wide downland panorama extending from the scrub covered slopes of High and Over on the left to the distinctive profile of Firle Beacon, away to the right.*

On reaching a road, turn left and, after about a quarter of a mile **(2)***, go right along a path signposted to Lullington Church. Follow this path past the church, accessible via a short path to the right.*

Lullington church, no more than 16 feet square, must be one of the smallest in the country, though it is really no more than a portion of the chancel of a much larger structure. It stands in a lovely spot, surrounded by trees, overlooking the Cuckmere valley.

Beyond the church the path soon drops down along a field edge with a fine view of

Alfriston Church and The Cuckmere River.

Alfriston Church. At a road, go right and immediately left on a path which takes you to the Cuckmere River. The bridge ahead provides access into Alfriston.

Alfriston gets very crowded at weekends and during the summer but is a delight out of season. The church, one of several which has acquired a 'cathedral of the Downs' label, stands on a low mound overlooking the river and the village green. The nearby clergy house, is owned by the National Trust, and open during the summer months.

To continue the walk, do not cross the river bridge (3). Instead, turn left and follow a path along the raised near side river bank. You are now on the alternative footpath route of the South Downs Way which you will be following as far as Westdean. After a pleasant mile beside the river, just short of the next bridge over the Cuckmere, turn left on a path which takes you out to a road at Litlington. The 12th-14th century church is a short distance along the road to the left but the walk continues to the right past the Plough and Harrow pub.

After 100 yards or so (4), turn left along a lane and, and, very shortly, fork right through a swing gate. A worn path climbs a grassy slope and continues along a ridge with good views across the Cuckmere valley to the prominent white horse hill figure on the slopes of High and Over. Unlike the Long Man, this is a relatively modern artefact.

Alfriston Church and The Clergy House.

73

The path approaching Jevington.

The path drops down into Charleston Bottom where, at a T-junction you should turn left. Shortly, fork right up a flight of steps and go ahead along a wide forest track. Follow the South Downs Way signs with care, ignoring a right fork. A final right turn brings you quickly down to the village of Westdean. On reaching a lane, turn left past the church and the Old Parsonage.

Westdean is a tiny secluded village, without pub or shop, tucked down in a quiet valley surrounded by the woodland of Friston Forest. The church dates back to the 11th Century, and the parsonage, though much restored, from 1220. Inside the church, look out for a memorial bust of the first Lord Waverley by Epstein.

A few yards beyond the church **(5)**, turn left past a Forestry Commission notice 'Friston Forest' to follow an access drive and then a forest track. Just past a pole barrier, fork left, signposted to Jevington. Follow, in turn, without change of direction, a woodland path, a forest track and then a wide woodland ride, climbing through the forest. Pass straight across an open area with fine views on the left towards Lullington Heath (Walk 8) before re-entering woodland. Keep with the main track, climbing steadily and ignoring all side paths and crossing tracks.

At the top, leave the woodland, cross a gallop and go ahead along a track which drops downhill with Jevington soon in view ahead against a backdrop of Combe Hill (Walk 2) to the left and Willingdon Hill to the right (*Walk 13*) and, in between, the valley leading up towards Butts Brow.

Join the road at Jevington past a small car park and turn left. Shortly *(6)* go left along Church Lane. On reaching the church, turn right through the churchyard, passing to the right of the Church.

Jevington Church is a typically charming example of a downland church, with flint walls and a solid Saxon tower although, like many, it has been subject to 19th century restoration

Leave the churchyard through a centrally pivoted tapsell gate and follow a path out to rejoin the road through the village. Continue past the Eight Bells pub and after another 200 yards or so go left along Green Lane. Shortly, go right along a fenced grassy path, between paddocks. Beyond a gate head out across a field, aiming for a stile, in sight. Continue over more stiles to join an enclosed track and turn right.

Shortly fork left up a scrub covered bank and follow another fenced path between paddocks to join another enclosed track. Bear right for a few yards and fork left once more up the bank to a stile.

A notice and map indicates that you are now entering an open access area established under the Countryside Stewardship Scheme. Until at least September 2112, and possibly longer if the agreement with the farmer is renewed, this allows us to use a magnificent high level route, bearing left up to and along the ridge of Folkington Hill. I have marked this superb alternative on the sketch map but have not described as it is not guaranteed to be permanently available. Enjoy it while you can.

For the direct route using rights of way, head straight out across the open area to a stile, and a path which drops obliquely down a steep grassy bank. Your route should be marked out as it heads out across a field to a fence corner and then bears right down to a T-junction with a track in front of a line of trees (7). Turn left to follow this track past the end of the cul-de-sac road at Folkington, next to the church. Continue along this track, part of the old coach road, along the patchily wooded foothills of the downland escarpment, high enough to give good views out across the Weald. You will pass a bridle gate on the left (8), where users of the high level route rejoin the main walk. Continue for another half a mile or so back to Wilmington, joining the village street opposite the church.

The tiny flint church, incorporates fragments from five Centuries. In the churchyard stands (just about) a much propped up yew tree which may be over 1000 years old. Inside, in the North Chapel, seek out a window, depicting 10 species of butterfly and moth including, including some now extinct.

Turn left back to the car park.

Walk 15
THE SOUTH DOWNS WAY, BISHOPSTONE AND FIRLE BEACON

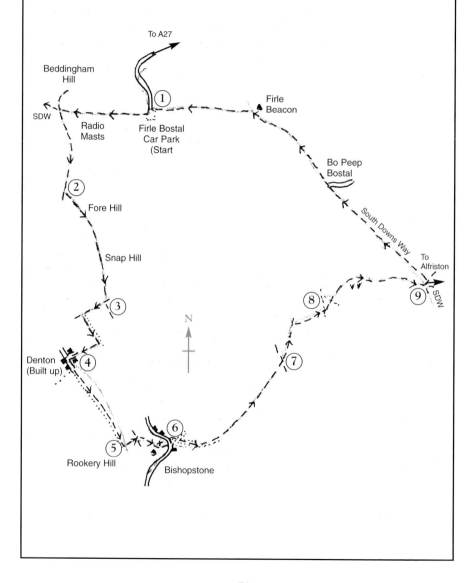

To A27

Beddingham Hill

SDW

Radio Masts

Firle Bostal Car Park (Start

Firle Beacon

Bo Peep Bostal

South Downs Way

To Alfriston

SDW

Fore Hill

Snap Hill

N

Denton (Built up)

Rookery Hill

Bishopstone

Walk 15
THE SOUTH DOWNS WAY, BISHOPSTONE AND FIRLE BEACON

Distance:	11¹/₄ miles.
Route:	Firle Bostal - Beddingham Hill - Fore Hill - Denton - Rookery Hill - Bishopstone - Hobbs Hawth - Greenway Bottom - South Downs Way - Firle Beacon - Firle Bostal.
Map:	OS Explorer 123: South Downs Way - Newhaven to Eastbourne.
Start/Parking:	From the A27 Lewes-to-Eastbourne road, about four miles east of Lewes follow the lane signposted to Firle. Keep right twice and follow the narrow bostal road up to the top of the Downs where there is a car park at GR 468059.
Public Transport:	None.
Conditions:	Good walking, mostly on chalk and flint tracks or across open downland. Several ups and downs, all well graded except for the steep descent from Rookery Hill.
Refreshments:	None on the route. Pub at Firle. All facilities at Alfriston, half a mile off the route.

This is an exhilarating airy walk, almost entirely on the bare open hills which, for many, define the character of the East Sussex Downs. The walk starts at the top of the northern downs escarpment and soon heads south across the undulating dip slope of the Downs where it is at its narrowest to the north of Newhaven and Seaford. Although longer than most walks in this book, the 'going' is generally good and you should cover the ground easily. For much of the walk you will be exposed to the prevailing wind, so go well clad if wind or rain are forecast. For the final stage of the walk you can enjoy one of the best stretches of the South Downs Way, within a generous swathe of close cropped pasture, rising to the summit of Firle Beacon, a fine climax to the walk.

THE WALK

From the Firle Bostal car park **(1)**, head westwards along the South Downs Way towards the radio masts on Beddingham Hill. About 200 yards beyond the masts and just short of a cattle grid, turn sharply back to the left across a field, heading for a gate. Continue in the same direction along the left edge of another field. Where the track divides **(2)**, fork left, up and over the left shoulder of Fore Hill, through a shallow dip and on over Snap Hill.

On reaching a crossing track **(3)**, turn right, climbing at first, then dropping down with the built up area of Denton directly ahead. About 60 yards beyond the highest point, turn left along a wide fenced track which climbs again and continues along the ridge of Norton Hill with a fence on the left. When you are alongside a gate and stile in this fence, turn right on a wide well ridden unfenced track.

At the edge of Denton **(4)**, go ahead along a rough access road (Palmerston Road) and at a T-junction, go left along an estate road (Falaise Road). Where this ends, go ahead on a clear path which passes through a dip and climbs again. Beyond a stile beside a gate, go ahead along the ridge with a fence on your right and a good view across Newhaven Harbour. In the field corner go forward over two stiles and continue along a right field edge, climbing almost to the top of Rookery Hill.

Where the ground begins to level out, just short of two grass covered tumuli **(5)** turn squarely left to a stile and drop steeply down the slope, across rough grass and through trees to find the next stile. Go over a crossing path, forward through a swing gate and on beside a flint wall to a second swing gate. Now bear half right across a meadow, aiming for Bishopstone Church. At a drive, go left and, shortly, right. After a few more yards go left up steps and across grass to enter Bishopstone churchyard.

Bishopstone, like Westdean (Walk 14), is a quiet unspoilt village with neither shop or pub. The village boasts one of the best preserved of all downland churches, much of it

Bishopstone Church Porch and Saxon Sundial.

78

of Saxon origin. The distinctive early Norman flint tower rises in four stages, crowned by a pyramidal spire. Over the porch is a Saxon sundial, carved with the name Eadric who may have been either the mason or the donor. Inside, if open (it was locked when I was last there), look for a fine carved 12th century coffin slab, built into the south wall of the tower.

Skirt to the left of the church, go right along the church access drive out a lane and turn left. After a few yards (6), go right along an unmade track, signposted as a public bridleway to East Blatchington. Ignore the first left fork. Where the main track veers right, you should fork left along an enclosed path which soon opens out as a terrace which contours along the hillside, gaining height gradually. A clear headland path continues along the right edge of three fields, eventually running parallel to a concrete drive on the right, which should be ignored. Join a wide bridleway coming in from the right and bear left along it between thickets. Go straight across a wide crossing track (7) and through a bridle gate, opposite. A path now drops obliquely down a scrub covered hillside.

At the bottom, where you have a choice of waymarked bridleways, fork right along a rather vague unfenced path which climbs gradually along the floor of a valley, Greenway Bottom. Beyond an unploughed patch up the hill to your right, a waypost guides you up the right side of the valley. At the top, go through a gate (8).

The stile on the right provides access to the Countryside Stewardship public access area of France Bottom. Although not included in this walk and not marked on OS maps, it is open for walkers, like Folkington Hill (Walk 14) at least until the agreement runs out in 2112, and provides superb walking.

To continue the present walk, ignore the stile and go forward with a fence to the right, Beyond a second gate go half right down into a valley and climb again, bearing right above a scrub covered hillside. On reaching a junction of several tracks (9), turn sharply left along the South Downs Way. (If in need of sustenance, Alfriston is now half a mile down the hill along the South Downs Way in the other direction - return the same way). To complete the walk you should now follow the South Downs Way generally westwards for about three miles. It passes the top of the Bo-peep Bostal road and climbs to the summit of Firle Beacon.

Firle Beacon, at over 700 feet above sea level, provides one of the finest viewpoints on the South Downs. To the northeast, the detached area of downland crowned by Mount Caburn (Walk 9) appears quite modest in height. To the west on the other side of the Ouse valley, the Downs escarpment stretches away as far as Ditchling Beacon (Walks 5 and 12). Southwards is Seaford and a wide expanse of the English Channel. Eastwards is Windover Hill (Walk 14) and the landward side of the coastline with the back view of Seaford Head and the first of the Seven Sisters clearly identifiable. Best of all, to the north, you can enjoy, on a clear day, a fine prospect across the Weald to the distant heights of Ashdown Forest.

Continue along the South Downs Way back to the start.

Walk 16
ROTTINGDEAN, KINGSTON AND TELSCOMBE

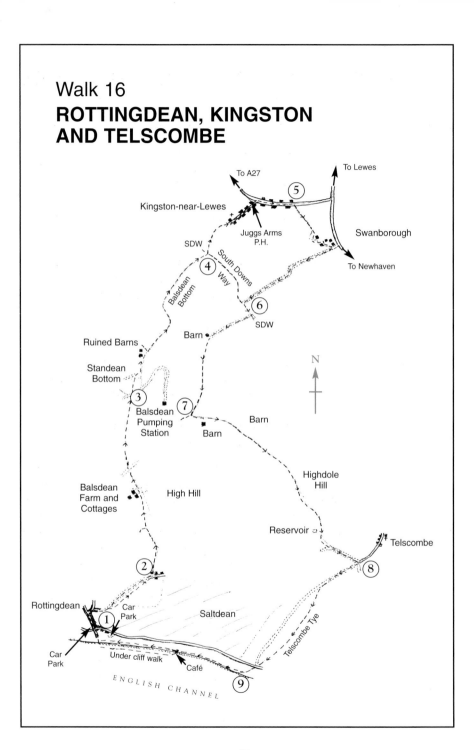

To A27

To Lewes

Kingston-near-Lewes

5

Swanborough

SDW

Juggs Arms P.H.

4

South Downs Way

To Newhaven

Balsdean Bottom

6

SDW

Ruined Barns

Barn

Standean Bottom

3

Balsdean Pumping Station

7

Barn

N

Barn

Balsdean Farm and Cottages

High Hill

Highdole Hill

Reservoir

Telscombe

8

2

Rottingdean

Car Park

Saltdean

Telscombe Tye

1

Car Park

Under cliff walk

Café

9

ENGLISH CHANNEL

Walk 16
ROTTINGDEAN, KINGSTON AND TELSCOMBE

Distance:	12 miles (12^1/$_2$ miles including detour to Telscombe village).
Route:	Rottingdean - Standean Bottom - Balsdean Bottom - Kingston Hill - Kingston - Swanborough - Swanborough Hill - Highdole Hill - Telscombe Tye - Rottingdean.
Map:	OS Explorer 122: South Downs Way - Steyning to Newhaven.
Start/Parking:	Rottingdean; car park beside the sea front road junction or between the A259 and the cliff edge about 200 yards up the hill to the east of the road junction (GR 371021).
Public Transport:	Frequent bus service from Brighton.
Conditions:	Good easy walking, much of it on clear tracks across high open downland. One steep, and sometimes, slippery descent to Kingston. One path which may be ploughed out.
Refreshments:	Pubs and teashops at Rottingdean; pub at Kingston; no facilities at Telscombe, café at Saltdean sea front (seasonal).

Starting from the coast at Rottingdean, this walk makes steady progress northwards across the rolling dip slope of the Downs before dropping down steeply to visit the villages of Kingston and Swanborough. After a steady climb back up to the top of the escarpment, it crosses more open downland with superb views all the way. After passing within easy reach of the secluded village of Telscombe, the walk returns to the sea, using the one undeveloped break in the urban coastal strip between Brighton and Newhaven, across the protected downland of Telscombe Tye. It then follows the coast back to Rottingdean where, for part of the distance you have a choice of paths either along the top or at the foot of high chalk cliffs.

Rottingdean is well worth exploring before or after the walk. It offers an attractive nucleus of fine houses clustered near the village green and pond. Rudyard Kipling occupied the Elms, next to the green, between 1897 and 1902. North End House, nearby was the home of the artist, Edward Burne-Jones in the late 19th Century. He designed some of the stained glass windows, made by William Morris, in Rottingdean Church. The Grange, a former vicarage, which now houses the Public Library and Museum, is also a fine 18th Century house.

THE WALK

Start the walk, heading away from the sea along Rottingdean High Street (1). Take the second turning on the right (Vicarage Lane), and then go first right along Whiteway Lane which continues as a rough track. Where this track divides, either will do, but the right hand, higher, path is the better of the two. Both will bring you out to the end of an estate road on the edge of Saltdean (Bishopstone Drive).

Go forward along the road for 30 yards only before turning left along a roughly metalled track which starts between bungalows numbered 50 and 52 (2). Follow this well worn bridleway up and along the ridge of High Hill, eventually passing to the right of the farm and cottages at Balsdean Farm. Beyond the farm, go through a bridle gate and ahead across open ground past a way post to join the access drive to Balsdean pumping station. Go through the gate opposite. To your right you will see three power poles in line abreast and you should aim for the one in the middle. About 50 yards beyond this power pole, pick up and follow a fence, left, along the upper hillside. In the field corner, cross a stile and maintain direction, aiming for the next stile, in sight. The path may be ploughed out without reinstatement and therefore not obvious.

In the next field cross a track, continue past a way post and down into Standean Bottom, one of the most delightful of all downland valleys, totally secluded though less than a mile from the built up area of Woodingdean.

At the bottom (3) join a track coming in from behind on your left, go forward for a few yards to a Y-junction and fork left. Now follow a track along the valley floor, skirt to the right of a group of ruined barns, go through a bridle gate and turn, right with a fence on your right. Ignore a signed path to the left along another valley (Falmer Bottom). Instead go ahead through a bridle gate and along a path which climbs very gradually along the floor of the main valley (Balsdean Bottom). Beyond another barn a solid track continues up to the head of the valley.

At the top (4), go straight across the South Downs Way and bear half right down the start of a terrace track. After about 15 yards only, turn left, dropping down along a narrower terrace with the village of Kingston directly ahead. The path steepens and brings you down through a belt of scrub to the village of Kingston.

Kingston-near-Lewes, named thus to distinguish it from another Kingston, near

The path down to Standean Bottom.

Rottingdean.

Rottingdean Church.

Telscombe Village.

Mount Caburn from Swanborough Hill.

Shoreham) is a prosperous village with an attractive 14th century church, and several old houses, notably the half timbered Kingston Manor, behind the church, dating from 1538.

Follow the village street to the road junction by the Juggs Arms pub and turn right. After about 350 yards (5) turn right again along a narrow path, signposted to Swanborough, 1 mile. Once out into a field keep along the left field edge, then pass through the farm buildings, veering left and on to join a metalled drive. Turn sharply right and head for the Downs.

After 650 yards, where you have a choice of signed bridleways, turn sharply back to the left along a concrete track which soon turns right and heads for the ridge of the Downs once more. Beyond a cattle grid, go ahead up to the ridge where a glance back provides one of the best views of Mount Caburn and the hills above Lewes.

At the top of Swanborough Hill (6), turn left along the edge of the escarpment. After 150 yards, go right through a bridle gate, and shortly go ahead along a concrete track. Skirt to the left of an isolated barn. A track continues along a high ridge and then begins to drop down. After about three quarters of a mile (7), at a Y-junction, fork left on a clear track which passes well to the left of a barn and to the right of a second barn as it climbs up on to Highdole Hill.

After a little over a mile, pass through a bridle gate to the right of a cattle grid and continue with a fence, right, along the ridge. The village of Telscombe is now in view, nestling down amongst the trees to your left. Turn left along the unmade drive from an isolated house and follow it out to the end of the road coming up from Telscombe where you should turn right (8).

Telscombe, worth the short detour from the main route of the walk, has resisted all pressures for road access from the coast and is the better for it, remaining a quiet backwater, tucked down among trees in a fold of the downs. It owes much of its tranquillity to Ambrose Goreham, a local benefactor. When he died in 1933, he bequeathed much of the village and its surroundings to Brighton Corporation. Trustees, who are bound by strict conditions designed to preserve the village and its rural surroundings, now manage the land. The church (which is normally locked) stands on a mound beside the road and is mostly Norman in origin.

Where the road coming up from Telscombe ends, go straight on along a track across Telscombe Tye, an open access area on which you can wander freely. Take your choice of route, heading for the sea, parallel to the track, with Saltdean spread out down the hill to your right. Cross the coast road, walk out to the edge of the cliff (9) and turn right. You can now follow the cliff top path to Rottingdean. Beyond Saltdean, as an alternative, you can follow the undercliff walk, which should be avoided in rough weather, particularly at high tide.

Walk 17
PLUMPTON PLAIN, NEWMARKET HILL AND BLACKCAP

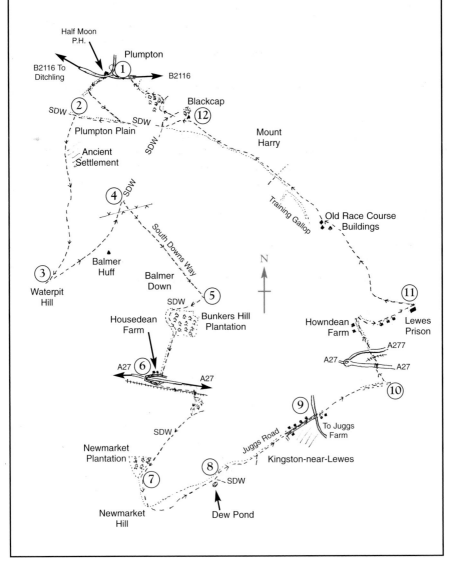

Walk 17
PLUMPTON PLAIN, NEWMARKET HILL AND BLACKCAP

Distance:	14 miles.
Route:	Plumpton - Plumpton Plain -Waterpit Hill - Balmer Down - South Downs Way - Newmarket Hill - Kingston Ridge - (edge of) Kingston - Houndean Bottom - Blackcap - Plumpton.
Map:	OS Explorer 122: South Downs Way - Steyning to Newhaven.
Start/Parking:	At Plumpton on the B2116 underhill road between Ditchling and Lewes. There is room to park in a lay by a few yards along Plumpton Lane which heads north from the B road beside the Half Moon Inn at Plumpton.
Public Transport:	Irregular bus service from Lewes.
Conditions:	Mostly good unimpeded walking along downland tracks, many of which are bridleways and may be churned up and muddy after rain. Several ups and downs.
Refreshments:	Half Moon, Plumpton at the start; Juggs Arms at Kingston, a quarter mile off the route.

Starting from Plumpton at the foot of the northern downs escarpment, this walk climbs quickly to the summit of the Downs. From here most of the circuit traverses high open downland with spectacular views. A new safe crossing, carrying the South Downs Way across the A27 allows us to follow the splendid ridge between Newmarket Hill and Kingston Ridge on the other side of the valley. After skirting the village of Kingston, we recross the A27 using another convenient bridge and climb steadily back up to the top of the Downs where the summit of Blackcap, now a fine open National Trust area, provides a fitting climax to the walk.

THE WALK

From the lay-by *(1)* return to the B2116 and follow a signed bridleway opposite (Plumpton Bostal). About half way up the hill, turn left through a bridle gate, doubling back on a path which climbs steps and heads steeply up a grassy terrace with a view northwards across the Weald to the distant heights of Ashdown Forest.

The path narrows as it curves along the rim of a steep combe and climbs to the summit of the escarpment. At the top, double back to the right along the South Downs Way which follows a clear track. After 700 yards *(2)*, turn left along another track, signed as a bridleway, which heads south, passing to the right of an unploughed area marked on the map as an ancient settlement. An unfenced track continues across high open downland.

From this path you get a good view, over to the left, of Firle Beacon and Mount Caburn, facing each other across the valley, and ahead to the ridge of the Downs above Kingston on to which you will be climbing later in the walk.

The track eventually crosses a valley and bears right to climb obliquely up the other side. At the top of the hill, go through a bridle gate *(3)* and double back to the left on a fenced track which takes a level course along the hill side. After a little over a mile *(4)*, about 100 yards after passing beneath power lines, double back to the right, now on the South Downs Way which you can follow gently down a long ridge.

On reaching a stile *(5)*, where the former route of the South Downs Way goes directly ahead, you should turn right through a bridle gate and follow the new route of the South Downs Way, tiresomely confined between fences, down into a valley. It then climbs on a poorly graded path up through Bunkers Hill Plantation and continues on a headland which takes you down towards the A27.

Just short of the main road, turn right and follow the South Downs Way past Housedean Farm, up and over the A27 *(6)* and back down the slip road on the other side. Where this road bears left to join the A27 carriageway, go ahead through a bridle gate and along a fenced path beside the railway embankment. After 600 yards, go right under the railway and follow a path which skirts along the foot of a wooded bank before climbing through the trees. Rejoin the old route of the South Downs Way and bear right to climb steadily with a fence and hedge on your right.

Towards the top of the hill the path opens out within a wide grassy strip and passes to the left of the battered remains of Newmarket Plantation, destroyed in the Great Gale of 1987. At the far end of the clump you have a choice of two gates*(7)*. Go through the one on the left and continue with the South Downs Way gently up along a right field edge through two more gates, bearing left to open out on to a wide grassy area.

Go ahead along this downland ridge, a fine unrestricted traverse with glorious views across the valley to the left. Converge gradually on the fence to your left. Beyond a stile and bridle gate in line abreast *(8)* where there is a nicely preserved dewpond on the right, the South Downs Way bears right. You, however, should go ahead, signposted Juggs Road, keeping a fence on your left.

The name is derived from the nickname 'Jug' given to Brighton fishermen. It was once the old route between Brighton and Lewes over the Downs and was used by Brighton fishwives to bring their husbands' catch for sale in Lewes.

You are soon on a substantial track which drops down, skirting round the shoulder of the hill with Kingston directly ahead. At the edge of the village go ahead along a road to reach Ashcombe Lane **(9)**. If in need of refreshment, the Juggs Arms is now a few minutes away along the lane to the right, returning the same way. The walk continues along the No Through Road opposite which, beyond houses, dwindles to a track and continues along a ridge, not particularly high but with some of the best views of the Caburn outlier, Firle Beacon and back to the ridge above Kingston.

A fenced path continues, skirting to the right of smallholdings. After about a quarter of a mile **(10)**, at the end of the last field on your right before the start of the built up area turn left where a waypost indicates a footpath. Go through a swing gate, and bear half left down across a field. Cross a bridge over the Lewes bypass, pass under the railway and continue to reach the A277. Follow the access drive to Houndean Farm, opposite. A track skirts to the right of the farm buildings. Very shortly past the farm, at a junction, turn sharply back to the right, uphill. Go straight over a crossing path and continue along a track with a housing estate to your right and rough pasture to your left.

On reaching a junction with another track, with the high wall of Lewes Prison away to your right **(11)**, you should double back to the left on a track which gains height steadily between areas of scrub and rough pasture. Pass to the right of the old Lewes racecourse buildings, now a residential development, out of keeping with this downland setting. A clear track continues, soon running parallel and to the right of a training gallop.

Ignore a left fork, go forward beneath power lines, through a gate and out on to the open National Trust area of Blackcap. An unfenced track continues across an open grassy area on the flank of Mount Harry and on up to the trig point on the summit of Blackcap **(12)**. At 600 feet above sea level this is the highest point on the walk and is an exceptional view point. The clump of trees, replanted some years ago, is now maturing. Each year it looks more and more like Chanctonbury Ring, once Sussex's most recognisable landmark until destroyed by gales in 1987.

Carry on past the trig point and the clump until you get to a gate and a National Trust notice. Don't go through this gate. Instead, turn sharply back to the right with a fence on your left and follow a track which descends between grassy banks. After about 200 yards, at a waypost, turn sharply back to the left on another fine sunken terraced path. Ignore a signed path which forks right and continue downhill through trees.

Towards the bottom of the hill a waypost with a yellow arrow directs you left to a stile from which a path crosses two fields to join the B2116. Turn left beside the road where there is a good path segregated from the carriageway at first. Within a few minutes you will be back at the Half Moon pub.

The track down to Plumpton.

Walk 18
CLAYTON, PYECOMBE AND LOWER STANDEAN

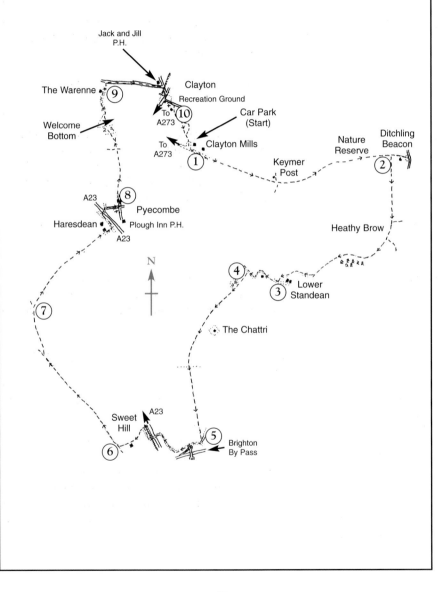

Jack and Jill P.H.

The Warenne

9

Clayton
Recreation Ground

Welcome Bottom

To A273

10

Car Park (Start)

To A273

Clayton Mills

Nature Reserve

Ditchling Beacon

1

Keymer Post

2

A23

8

Pyecombe

Haresdean

Plough Inn P.H.

A23

Heathy Brow

N

4

Lower Standean

3

7

The Chattri

Sweet Hill

A23

6

5

Brighton By Pass

Walk 18
CLAYTON, PYECOMBE
AND LOWER STANDEAN

Distance:	11 miles.
Route:	Clayton Mills - Ditchling Beacon - Lower Standean - Waterhall - East Hill - Pyecombe - Wellcombe Bottom - Clayton - Clayton Mills.
Map:	OS Explorer 122: South Downs Way - Steyning to Newhaven.
Start/Parking:	At Clayton Mills, which are signposted along a lane from the top of Clayton Hill on the A273 Pyecombe-to-Hassocks road. The car park is next to the mills at GR 303134. Jack Windmill is normally open on Sundays between April and September from 2 to 5.
Public Transport:	Bus from Brighton to Pyecombe, joining the walk at point 8.
Conditions:	Mostly easy walking along chalk and flint tracks through moderately hilly terrain. Gentle gradients except for one steep descent into Wellcombe Bottom which can be slippery after rain.
Refreshments:	Plough Inn at Pyecombe, just off the route. Jack and Jill pub at Clayton.

Although mostly within East Sussex, this walk starts and finishes in West Sussex and also strays over the county boundary into the administrative area of the Brighton and Hove Unitary Authority. Apart from a noisy crossing of the A23 and a short section beside the Brighton bypass, it is a quiet and unspoilt walk across surprisingly remote and unpopulated downland. Let us hope this tranquillity can be preserved in the face of ever present risks of development extending north from Brighton and Hove, bursting at the seams and hungry to extend into the Downs if permitted to do so.

THE WALK

From the entrance to the car park (1), turn left along a wide unmade track, passing Jack Mill away to your left. After about 200 yards, fork left, climbing gently, now on the South Downs Way which you will be following almost to Ditchling Beacon. The track rises for a little over half a mile to reach Keymer Post, first carved and erected by local school children and recently refurbished. Beyond the post, the official route keeps to the right of the fence ahead, eventually opening out on to a broad grassy area, part of a nature reserve managed by the Sussex Wildlife Trust. Walk beside the fence along the right edge of this area until, about 200 yards short of the summit of Ditchling Beacon, you should turn right through a bridle gate, signposted to Heathy Brow (2).

The short extension up to the trig point on the top of Ditchling Beacon is well worth the minor effort necessary. At 813 feet above sea level, it is the highest point on the East Sussex Downs with a 360 degree view. On a clear day you should be able to pick out Betchworth Quarry on the North Downs. Westwards, various points along the escarpment are identifiable, notably Truleigh Hill and Chanctonbury Ring. To the east you can see as far as Firle Beacon (Walk 15) and Windover Hill (Walk 14) and along the Heritage Coast where the notched outlines of the back view of Seaford Head and the first of the Seven Sisters beyond Cuckmere Haven are recognisable.

Follow the Heathy Brow bridleway southwards, unfenced between arable fields at first, then as a fenced track which begins to drop down into a valley. Where the enclosed track opens out, go forward on a faint path which winds along the floor of the valley (North Bottom). Walk parallel to the fence on your right at first until you can use a bridle gate to get through this fence and continue with it on your left. Shortly a more substantial track diverts to the right of the fence to climb over the shoulder of a hill and down to Lower

Standean where it reaches a T-junction to the right of the farm buildings (3). (NB the signposted bridleway differs considerably from the right of way as marked on OS maps).

Turn right, and follow a track which climbs out of the valley. On reaching a gate and a barn, go ahead, keeping to the right of the fence ahead rather than along the track. Beyond a bridle gate, turn left and follow a defined track once

Keymer Post.

more. *Where the ground levels out (4), turn left through a bridle gate and follow an unfenced track across high open downland, passing to the left of an isolated tree clump and onward with a fence on your right.*

Beyond the next bridle gate you can divert a short distance down the hill to visit the Chattri. Carved from Sicilian marble and erected in 1921, it commemorates the Indian

The Chattri.

soldiers who died during World War I and were cremated on this site. It is surrounded by a landscaped area with full public access, and is a lovely tranquil spot in a beautiful downland setting.

Continue gently down a long ridge, walking parallel to the fence on the right. At the far end of two fields, join an access lane and go forward for 10 yards to a T-junction, with the noisy Brighton bypass directly ahead (5). Turn right here. Skirt to the right of a roundabout and follow an access road running parallel to the bypass slip road at first. After a little over a quarter of a mile, at a waypost, turn left across a footbridge over the A23 and the railway, following the path round to the right on the other side of the bridge.

At a junction with a track coming over the railway from the right, turn left between concrete posts and go right along a rough access track which climbs up on to Sweet Hill where the roar of traffic on the A23 quickly recedes. At a T-junction at the top of the hill (6), turn right on a fenced track

You will soon pass, on the right, a dewpond where a notice provides a brief account of the original construction methods used to create these traditional downland features. The dewpond was once an essential requirement for the supply of water for sheep and cattle in this dry landscape. Now most are redundant and have fallen into decay.

Follow the main track for more than a mile, gaining height gradually along the ridge of Varncombe Hill and up on to the more open area of East Hill. About 60 yards beyond a bridle gate you will come to a waypost offering a choice of bridleways (7). Fork right here, indicated as part of the North Brighton Countryside Trail. An unfenced track now takes you up and over the shoulder of West Hill and down towards Pyecombe.

As you begin to descend, a wide view opens out ahead to Pyecombe and your final destination, the twin mills of Jack and Jill. Over to the left is Wolstonbury

Pyecombe Church.

Clayton Village from Clayton Hill.

Beacon and a wedge of the distant Weald through the gap between Wolstonbury and Newtimber Hill.

Go through a double gate and drop downhill with a fence on your right and the village of Pyecombe and Clayton Mills directly in line ahead. At the bottom go forward along an access drive, following it left and right across a bridge over the A23. On the other side of the bridge turn right between concrete posts and walk up to Pyecombe Church.

Access to the churchyard is through a tapsell gate, adorned with a replica of the head of the famous Pyecombe Shepherd's Crook, once made in the old forge, opposite the church. Inside the church, note the rare Norman lead font, dating from 1170 when the church was built.

*Just past the church **(8)**, if in need of refreshment, the Plough Inn is along the lane to the right. Our walk continues along the No Through Road to the left called The Wyshe, which soon narrows to a bridleway and climbs between hedged banks. It is difficult to imagine that this was once part of the main Brighton-to-London coach road.*

At the top of the slope, where several tracks meet, go straight ahead, passing to the right of a National Trust notice 'Wolstonbury Hill'. A track with a fence, left, begins to drop downhill with a view of Wolstonbury away to the left. After less than a 100 yards, go left over a stile and cross a field corner to the next stile. A path now drops steeply down through woodland, slippery in places, though there are steps to help you down the steepest bit. Go straight over a crossing bridleway, leave the wood over a stile and go ahead over a field, crossing Wellcombe Bottom and climbing to join and follow a fence, left.

*Go through a squeeze stile and ahead, downhill, along a wide track which takes you past a cottage called The Warenne and out via the cottage drive to New Way Lane **(9)** where you should turn right. Follow this lane for almost half a mile out to the A273, where the Jack and Jill pub is a few yards to the left. Turn right across the railway with a good view of the castellated entrance to Clayton Tunnel, dating from 1844 in the 'golden age' of the railways. Take the second turning on the left, Underhill Lane, soon passing Clayton Church on your right.*

The church, of Saxon origins, is notable for a remarkable set of wall paintings, executed an about 1150, probably by a monk from the Benedictine priory at Lewes. They depict the Last Judgement.

*After another 100 yards or so **(10)**, turn right beside the gateway to Clayton Court Stables and go ahead along a heavily used bridleway. Once through a bridle gate on to open grass downland, you have a choice of signed footpath and bridleway. The footpath is the best option, bearing half left and climbing steadily on a grassy terrace. Bridleway and footpath rejoin and head for Clayton Mills now in sight on the skyline. A short climb brings you back to the start*

ABOUT THE AUTHOR

Ben Perkins was born in the village of Rodmell, near Lewes and has lived, worked and walked in Sussex throughout his life. He is a keen conservationist and long standing member of the Society of Sussex Downsmen, Society of Sussex Wealdmen and the Rambler's Association. Over the last 15 years he has contributed more than 400 walk descriptions to a regular column in the Brighton Evening Argus and, during that time has managed to explore much of the 2000 mile network of local footpaths and bridleways.

S.B. Publications publish a wide range of local interest books on Sussex.
For a free catalogue please write to:
S.B. Publications, 19 Grove Road, Seaford, East Sussex BN25 1TP
or access our website on
www.sbpublications.swinternet.co.uk